THE GRESFORD LETTERS

Aftermath of a Mining Disaster

Letters, Love and Loyalty in 1934

Beverley Tinson

middle view

THE GRESFORD LETTERS

Aftermath of a Mining Disaster.

Letters, Love and Loyalty in 1934

© 2009 Beverley Tinson MA

ISBN 978-1-902964-11-9

Published by Middleview

an imprint of Avid Publications
Middleview, New Road,
GWESPYR
Flintshire. U.K
CH8 9LS
Tel : (44) 01745 886769
e-mail: info@AvidPublications.co.uk

Other publications available from Avid / Middleview are detailed
at the rear of this book

FOR MARTIN, LINDSAY & STEWART

and Grandchildren
Lois and Gwilym Roberts
with love

**In memory of the 266 miners who died at
Gresford Colliery, September 1934,
Ithel Kelly and Blodwen Bryan**

The Gresford Disaster - a Ballad

You've heard of the Gresford Disaster
And the terrible price that was paid
Two hundred and forty two colliers were lost
And three men of the rescue brigade

It occurred in the month of September
At three in the morning, that pit
Was racked by a violent explosion
In the Dennis where gas lay so thick

The gas in the Dennis deep section
Was packed like snow in a drift
And many a man had to leave the coal-face
Before he had worked out his shift

A fortnight before the explosion
To the shotfirer, Tomlinson cried:
If you fire that shot we'll all be blown to Hell
And no one can say that he lied

The fireman's reports they are missing
The records of forty-two days;
The colliery manager had them destroyed
To cover his criminal ways

Down there in the dark they are lying
They died for nine shilling a day
They have worked out their shift and now hey must lie
In the darkness until Judgement Day

The Lord Mayor of London's collecting
To help both our children and wives
The owners have sent some white lilies
To pay for the poor colliers lives

Farewell our dear wives and our children
Farewell, our old comrades as well
Don't send your sons down the dark dreary pit;
They'll be damned like the sinners in Hell

ANONYMOUS

(The italics highlight the parts which are dubious in their origin or fact.)

"There were those who were dead against the management and those who were dead against the workmen. You have to tell the truth as you see it, from the facts, warts and all. If you are going to do it, do it right. We have a responsibility, you and I, unless it is a novel you are writing, to tell the facts, so that people who come, after you and I have gone, can get the facts of what happened - not a one-sided lefty view." -

Advice to the author in 1996 from Ithel Kelly - the last underground manager at Gresford Colliery.

Gresford Colliery Disaster

Once more in North Wales
in the morning
A great loss of lives in the mine,
Struck Dead in their prime
without warning,
Struck Dead in a moment of time,
They say about two hundred and
sixty,
The young and the aged as well,
At work underground,
A sad Death they found,
In the midst of their labour's
they fell.
        This Explosion is dreadful
to think of,
A discription Alas only fails,
These brave men and boys,
Torn away from Lifes joys,
At Gresford Colliery North Wales.

    Written By John Ellison
        Middle Spen Moor
            Radcliffe

A poem sent from John Ellison of Radcliffe, Lancashire, in the hope that his words may be sold to raise money for the relief fund.

Acknowledgements

I wish to thank my family first of all because they 'lived through' my study and research and the writing of this book. My husband Martin, and my children Lindsay and Stewart.
I love you all and could not have done it without you.
My tutor, supervisor, friend and colleague Joss West-Burnham, at MMU Cheshire.
Jenny Lee for all our 'chats' and support.
Hazel Kelly and Eirwen Williams.
Claire and all the staff at Flintshire Records Office
Rose Williams at Wrexham NUM
Chay Welford, Angela Dunn, Fiona George and Paul Williams my 'Uni Buddies.'
For all my students past and present - "If I can do it so can **YOU**!"
My publisher David Roberts for his patience and understanding and making 'IT' happen. Oh, and not forgetting his wife Denise for the cups of tea.
Alan Stone with thanks for all your encouragement.
Anne Horobin, former Mayor of Prestatyn for her advice.
Last but not least all those organisations and individuals and their loved ones listed here who supported me in making this work a reality. Bless your hearts.

P.J. - Corwen
Sophia Drew MBE. Prestatyn
Mrs Hazel Kelly, Pandy, Wrexham
Miss Sybil Jones, Pandy, Wrexham
The Vale Wordsmiths, Corwen
Kings Hall Writers, Prestatyn
H. Gethin Davies OBE, Llangollen
Peter Howell, Wrexham
The Reverend Canon David Griffiths.
Heather Roberts. Businesswork
Solutions Ltd.
Vernie & Lily Edwards and Mrs
Phyllis Parry in memory Ernest Monk,
lost at Gresford.
Tony Andrews, Gwynlys, Bwlchgwyn
Bill & Irene Cooper, West Parade, Rhyl
K J Bishop, Trained at Gresford
Emrys Davies, Ex Miner Gresford
In memory of Richard Arthur Griffiths
and Richard Albert Griffiths
Wrexham Conservative Association
Ruby McBurney & Majorie Morrison(d)
Ian Lucas, M. P. for Wrexham

Sylvia Habberley, in memory of John
David Rowlands and their Mother.
Gary Alexander, Marie Elizabeth,
Natashia Jane-Alexandra and Feelix
Bourne.
Mrs Jill Tyrer, Cefn Maen Isaf, Saron
Jenny Gilpin (Gill) Wrexham
Ian and Anne Chesterman, Wrexham
Rowena Thomas, Bwlchgwn
Gerald O'Leary, Denbigh
Denbigh & District Labour Party
Abergele Rotary Club
Wrexham Football Club
David Barry Roberts
Cyril Jones Solicitors, Wrexham
Mr & Mrs W.E. Rowley & Mr & Mrs J.
Price Jones (Grandchildren of George
Evans)
Jerry Allcock
Wrexham Borough Council
Rev. Eric Owen, Marford
Elfed Roberts, Trained at Gresford
Alun 'Ginger' Roberts, Gresford

CONTENTS

Men lost at Gresford Colliery, Denbighshire, September 1934

ANDERS, JOSEPH
ANDERS, JOHN
ANDERSON, GEORGE
ANDREWS, ALFRED OWEN
ARCHIBALD, JOSEPH
ARCHIBALD, THOMAS
BAINES, DAVID
BATEMAN, MALDWYN OWEN
BATHER, EDWARD WYNNE
BEDDOWS, EDWARD
BEW, ARTHUR
BEWLEY, THOMAS LLOYD
BOWEN, ALFRED
BOYCOTT, HARRY
BRAIN, HERBERT
BRAMWELL, GEORGE
BRANNAN, JOSEPH
BROWN, JOHN GEORGE WILLIAM
BROWN, WILLIAM ARTHUR
BRYAN, JOHN ARTHUR HENRY
BUCKLEY, ALBERT
BURNS, FREDERICK
CAPPER, JOHN ARTHUR
CARTWRIGHT, ALBERT EDWARD
CARTWRIGHT, CHARLES
CHADWICK, STEPHEN
CHESTERS, EDWIN
CLUTTON, ARTHUR
CLUTTON, GEORGE ALBERT
CLUTTON, JOHN THOMAS
COLLINS, JOHN
CORNWALL, THOMAS RICHARD
CRUMP, WILLIAM
DARLINGTON, THOMAS
DAVIES, ARTHUR
DAVIES, EDWARD

DAVIES, GEORGE WILLIAM
DAVIES, HUGH
DAVIES, JAMES (Brymbo)
DAVIES, JAMES (Moss)
DAVIES, JAMES EDWARD
DAVIES, JOHN (7 Maelor Place)
DAVIES, JOHN 'Fernleigh'
DAVIES, JOHN RALPH
DAVIES, JOHN EDWARD
DAVIES, PETER (New Rhosrobin)
DAVIES, PETER (Wrexham)
DAVIES, PETER (Bradley)
DAVIES, MATTHIAS
DAVIES, ROBERT THOMAS
DAVIES, SAMUEL
DAVIES, THOMAS
DAVIES, WILLIAM
DODD, THOMAS
DUCKETT, FREDERICK
EDGE, JOSEPH
EDGE, THOMAS SAMUEL
EDWARDS, ALBERT
EDWARDS, ENOCH GLYN
EDWARDS, ERNEST
EDWARDS, FRANK
EDWARDS, JAMES SAMUEL
EDWARDS, JOHN EDWARD
EDWARDS, JOSEPH CADWALLDR
EDWARDS, THOMAS DAVID
EDWARDS, THOMAS ERNEST
EDWARDS, WILLIAM
EDWARDSON, JOHN
ELLIS, GEORGE EDWARD
EVANS, FRED GEORGE
EVANS, JOSEPH
EVANS, NORMAN
EVANS, RALPH
FISHER, LEONARD
FOULKES, IRWIN
GABRIEL, RICHARD GEORGE

GITTINS, JOSEPH HENRY
GOODWIN, JOHN
GRIFFITHS, EDWARD
GRIFFITHS, EDWARD CHARLES
GRIFFITHS, ELLIS
GRIFFITHS, EMMANUEL
GRIFFITHS, JOHN FRANCIS
GRIFFITHS, WALTER
HALL, WALTER
HALLAM, THOMAS WALTER
HAMLINGTON, ARTHUR
HAMPSON, FRANK
HARRISON, ARTHUR
HARRISON. EDWARD
HEWITT, PHILLIP
HIGGINS, WILLIAM HENRY
HOLT, ALFRED
HOULDEN, HENRY JOHN
HUGHES, CECIL
HUGHES, DANIEL
HUGHES, OWEN
HUGHES, HARRY
HUGHES, JOHN
HUGHES, PETER JOSEPH
HUGHES, ROBERT JOHN
HUGHES, WALTER ELLIS
HUGHES, WILLIAM (Brymbo)
HUGHES, WILLIAM (New Rhosrobin)
HUMPHREYS, BENJAMIN
HUMPHREYS, JOSEPH
HUSBANDS, THOMAS
JARVIS, ERNEST
JENKINS, WILLIAM
JOHNS, PERCY
JONES, ALBERT EDWARD
JONES, AZARIAH
JONES, CYRIL
JONES, DANIEL
JONES, DAVID LLOYD
JONES, EDWARD (Gwersyllt)

JONES, EDWARD (Cefn)
JONES, EDWARD
GEORGE
JONES, ERIC
JONES, ERNEST
JONES, EVAN HUGH
JONES, FRANCIS
OWEN
JONES, FREDERICK,
JONES, FREDERICK
CYRIL
JONES, GEORGE
LLEWELYN
JONES, GEORGE
HUMPHREY
JONES, GWYLM PETER
JONES, HENRY
JONES, IDIRS
JONES, IOWERTH
JONES, JABEZ
JONES, JOHN
RICHARD
JONES, JOHN ROBERT
JONES, JOHN SAMUEL
JONES, LLEWELLYN
(Windsor Road)
JONES, LLEWELLYN
(Bersham Road)
JONES, LLEWELLYN
(Gresford)
JONES, NEVILLE
JONES, RICHARD
HENRY
JONES, RICHARD
JAMES
JONES, ROBERT
(Penycae)
JONES, ROBERT
(Gresford)
JONES, THOMAS
JONES, THOMAS
ENOCH
JONES, THOMAS JOHN
JONES, THOMAS
OWEN
JONES, WILLIAM (Rhos)
JONES, WILLIAM
(Rhosddu)
KELSALL, JAMES
KELSALL, JOHN
LAWRENCE, WILLIAM

LEE, JOHN THOMAS
LEE, THOMAS
LEWIS, DAVID THOMAS
LEWIS, DAVID
LEWIS, JOHN
LILLEY, JOEL
LLOYD, THOMAS
LLOYD, WILLIAM
LLOYD, WILLIAM
SIDNEY
LUCAS, JOHN
McKEAN, JOSEPH
MAGGS, COLIN VERDUN
MANNION, ALBERT
MANUEL, THOMAS
ARTHUR
MARTIN, WILLIAM
HENRY
MATHEWS, WILLIAM
VINCENT
MATTHIAS, SAMUEL
MEADE, WILLIAM
MITCHELL, GEORGE
MONK, ERNEST
MORLEY, EDWARD
MORRIS, ALFRED
NICHOLLS, HARRY
NICHOLLS, JOHN
NICHOLLS, WILLIAM
HENRY
OWENS, EVAN HENRY
PALMER, ALEX
PARRY, ISAAC
PARRY, JOHN EDWARD
PARRY, JOHN RICHARD
PARRY, JOSEPH
PENNY, STEVEN
PENNY, WILLIAM
HENRY
PERRIN, FRANK
CORBETT
PETERS, HENRY
PHILLIPS, GEORGE
PHILLIPS, HERBERT
PHILLIPS, JOHN
PICKERING, JOHN
FREDERICK
POWELL, CHARLES
PRICE, ERNEST
PRICE, SAMUEL
PRIDDING, JOSEPH

PRINCE, MARK
PRINCE, WILLIAM
PRITCHARD, ISIAH
PUGH, ERNEST
PUGH, THOMAS HENRY
RALPHS, JOHN
RANCE, THOMAS
RANDOLPH
READ, LLOYD
REES, ALBERT
ROBERTS, ARTHUR
ALLEN
ROBERTS, EDWARD
ROBERTS, EDWARD
COSTER
ROBERTS, ERNEST
ROBERTS, FRANK
ROBERTS, GEORGE
ROBERTS, IDRIS
ROBERTS, JOHN HENRY
ROBERTS, JOHN DAVID
ROBERTS, OLIVER
ROBERTS, PERCY
ROBERTS, ROBERT
ROBERTS, ROBERT JOHN
ROBERTS, ROBERT
THOMAS
ROBERTS, ROBERT
WILLIAM
ROBERTS, THOMAS
JAMES
ROBERTS, WILLIAM
ROBERTS, WILLIAM
HENRY
ROBERTSON, WILLIAM
ROGERS, EDWIN
LLEWELLYN
ROGERS, GRANVILLE
ROSS, HARRY
ROWLANDS, JOHN
ROWLANDS, JOHN
DAVID
SALISBURY, WILLIAM
SHAW, GEORGE
SHONE, JOHN
SHONE, RICHARD
SLAWSON, ARTHUR
SMITH, LEONARD
STEVENS, RICHARD
THOMAS
STRANGE, ALBERT

STRANGE, FREDERICK
STRATFORD, STANLEY
TARRAN, JOHN
TAYLOR, WILLIAM
HENRY
THOMAS, BERWYN
THOMAS, ERNEST
TECWYN
THOMAS, JOHN ELIAS
THOMAS, ROBERT
THORNTON, JOHN
TITTLE, RALPH
EDWARD
TROW, ERNEST
VALENTINE,
FREDERICK ARTHUR

VAUGHAN, JOHN
EDWARD
WHITE, JOHN
WILLIAMS, ARTHUR
REGINALD
WILLIAMS, GEORGE
WILLIAMS, HAROLD
WILLIAMS, HUGH LLOYD
WILLIAMS, JOHN (28 Dale
Street)
WILLIAMS, JOHN (Mount
Street)
WILLIAMS, JOHN DAVID
WILLIAMS, JOHN
THOMAS

WILLIAMS, JAS
WILLIAMS, NORRIS
WILLIAMS, THOMAS
WILLIAMS, WILLIAM
ARTHUR
WILSON, JOHN
WALTER
WINYARD, WALTER
WILLIAM
WITTER, HENRY
WYNNE, EDWARD
YEMM, MORGAN
JAMES

CHAPTER 1
Introduction

Whilst reading the history of a house, near to where I live in North Wales, on the outskirts of Coedpoeth near Wrexham, I came across the Gresford Mining Disaster of 1934 where 266 lives were lost. The extracts in italics that follow are an abridged version from a diary I kept and illustrate how I became interested in the 1934 coalmining disaster at Gresford and which became the impetus for this particular research.

Today I went to the Archives and asked where I could find information about the house 'Pwll Glo', (which from my Welsh dictionary means coalpit) on the outskirts of Coedpoeth near Wrexham. The archivist brought out the ordinance survey maps of the area and we found that the house was actually called Pwll y Go which means 'Pool of the Blacksmith.' The house itself is well documented in several books including one by the renowned historian, A. N. Palmer, and also in a book about the Ironworks at Bersham, the site of which is approximately half a mile across the fields behind Pwll y Go. The whole area has different mining connections, not only coal, but iron and various metals. The archivist also brought me numerous books about the coalfields of Denbighshire, which included histories of the areas.

The books made really interesting reading, the injustice of the mineworkers in the area, how they lived and in what harsh conditions they had to work. Then I read about the disaster at the Gresford mine, about five miles from Coedpoeth, in which 266 men and boys were killed. This was one of the biggest mining disasters in British coalmining history, second only to one in South Wales at Senghenydd, where the bodies also, were never recovered. Because men came from a large surrounding area, including Coedpoeth and other villages, many local families were affected. I have this overwhelming feeling of sadness, not only for the miners, but also for the women and the families left behind.

Collieries of Denbighshire. by G.G.Lerry, 1946, makes fascinating reading. It lists a number of collieries in alphabetical order, such as Bersham, Coedpoeth, Gresford, Llay Main, all within a ten mile radius of Coedpoeth. On reading the notes relating to each colliery I am really amazed at the things that went on there, that were allowed to go on there. The hours that these men worked, for the pittance they were paid, and the alleged injustice of their treatment by the mine-owners.... I am reminded of Richard Llewellyn's How Green is my Valley (1939) and the Novels of Wales (1987) by Alexander Cordell, where to be Welsh unless you owned the land, or the mines or quarries, meant a very hard life. However, these books were set in South Wales and not North Wales, so this disaster really interests me, not just for its fictional potential, to write a good story, but because of the history of something that happened on my own doorstep. Of all the mines in North Wales, Gresford is the one that people remember the most, or so I am told, because all those men died, needlessly. It must have been awful for the relatives not to have their bodies to bury, for they were entombed after the explosion, and not knowing how their men had died.

Once I had decided to use this mining disaster as a basis for research I spent weeks trawling through all the information I could find relating to Mines in the Wrexham area and started asking locally what was known about the Gresford disaster. Although this disaster happened over seventy-five years ago I was still able to find men and women, who knew someone connected with Gresford, and the library at Wrexham holds numerous files and has volumes of information relating specifically to Gresford Colliery and the disaster. Many Wrexhamites have their own family stories and can tell you **"what really happened"** The arguments and discussions continue to this day regarding the Colliery closure, the Relief Fund and the fate of the miner and his working conditions and *"about influence, about blame and judgement."*

I contacted the Mineworkers Union in Wrexham and they put me in touch with a man who was to become my "fountain of knowledge" - Ithel Kelly, a local historian and authority on the Gresford Colliery, having been the last acting manager there before the mine's closure. He in turn introduced me to Blodwen Bryan and her friend Mrs Williams; Blodwen at 96 years of age was one of the last surviving widows of the miners lost at Gresford Colliery and Mrs Williams' father had worked at Gresford at the time of the disaster. As a trustee of the Gresford Colliery Disaster Relief Fund Ithel Kelly was privy to all the documents relating to the Fund. The bulk of these documents are now kept at the Flintshire Records Office at Hawarden, which I was able to access on my countless visits to this office over a period of three years, reading numerous deeds, lists, newspapers, registers, minutes of meetings and over 10,000 letters, plus, Ithel Kelly made available to me, his own letters, papers and photographs collected in his time as the last acting manager at the Gresford Colliery.

My research has not had a natural progression. In the beginning I thought that it would be straightforward to work chronologically from the past to the present or visa versa. This was not possible, some of my information came from the most unlikeliest of sources and in the case of my interview with the 96 year old widow, I had to find ways to jog her memory to be assured that the reminiscences related to me were from the 1930's and not an earlier or later decade. Only by constantly retracing my steps and cross referencing my information was I convinced that the information I have is as accurate as possible, bearing in mind the period of time that has elapsed since the disaster at Gresford.

From the outset, even though in the beginning this research was for a degree, I wanted to share with everyone the information I was to uncover. It was important to me that the relatives left would know that all these people who wrote letters and gave donations felt the grief of their tragic loss, however belated. Without a blueprint guide, of the right way to conduct this research, I admit to stumbling across information by accident rather than design, which fortunately has led onto other related information. Not a textbook way of conducting research I grant you, but interesting and with the "ability to surprise."

It is the letters, written in response to the disaster from people from all walks of life, that have become the main focus of my research providing an invaluable insight into not only the lives and experiences of people living in the 1930's, but the history of the coalmining industry in North Wales. I see the "exploration" of relationships and experiences, albeit retrospectively and from texts (letters), as the basis of my book. The "mapping out" of the different series of overlaps and conjunctions, focusing on the Mining Disaster at Gresford, is my example of "the something at stake"[1]. Wanting to know more, is the "hook" I required, and unfolding the hidden stories of the ways in which other women chose to help the widows and their families, was the "something at stake" which propelled me on with this research.

The 'one great silent area' in all the accounts of the Gresford Mining Disaster is; what happened in the aftermath, of the disaster to the women and families of the miners who were killed? There is only so much one can write about dead miners, their bravery, their toil and the hardship of their working conditions, yet I was concerned to find out more about the women and the consequences for them of losing their men-folk. Central to this concern was a notion of 'experience', and to this end I concentrated on the letters.

I explored the novels of Raymond Williams, a Welshman from a working class background, familiar with the coal mining areas of South Wales. An academic who wrote reflexively and autobiographically of his feelings for Wales and his links with its rural communities, to find a "hook" that would help me define the women's experience in a coal mining area but found instead another silent area. (Williams' curious banishment of women from history and politics, and with only a fleeting mention, in his novels, is discussed by Jane Miller in her book 'Seductions'[2]. The words "hidden from"," silent area," and "from below", in relation to women and women's history, conjure up an aura of deliberateness, as if this was how it should be.

Are we too ready to jump to the conclusion that because something is/was not visible it was deliberately hidden? In the case of my research, especially the letters, I must then question that if the letters were not deliberately hidden away, why were they not made more visible? Was one of the reasons, that the knowledge contained in them was more than was publicly known, or on offer at the time and felt to be embarrassing or prejudicial in some way?

Over forty files containing over 10,000 letters and documents relating to the Gresford Relief Fund were held at the Mineworkers Union in Wrexham but were not transferred to the records office until the 1980's, after the pit closed for good. Who had access to these files during those fifty years? Who would have wanted to investigate them, and for what purpose? Would it have helped a bereaved family to see or read for themselves the extent to which people responded to their plight?

I would argue that the experiences and emotions expressed in these letters are the authenticating source of this book - the descriptive evidence of 'the already there,' rendering visible hitherto hidden lives and unacknowledged experiences[3]. Also that the 'mapping out' of different series of overlaps and conjunctions, the past with the present, the researcher with the research, the emotions engendered then and now, their differences and their similarities can be mobilized in a number of ways for different purposes and different knowledgeable outcomes. So that I as a researcher, can reflect/identify with the subject of research, as a woman, a mother and as a wife living and working in Wales.

This was no Hollywood How Green was my Valley (1941), no myth, fictionalised as a story, this was a Mining disaster that actually took place more than seventy-five years ago in North Wales. There was no village community, for the men came from all surrounding areas of Wrexham. There was no stereotypical Welsh MAM at the pit head like the one portrayed by the actress Rachel Roberts in the film How Green was my Valley, in a shawl with an ample bosom, surrounded by her daughters in law, waiting for news of her man and her big strapping sons. Although some did come and stand and wait they would have had to walk miles as only 14 of the miners came from Gresford village. The hooter would have sounded and been heard miles away but unlike the film portrayal, as it wasn't a pit village, they would not have come straight away or understand what had happened and why the hooter was going. Some like Blodwen Bryan did not know anything was wrong until the postman was making his deliveries and knocked on her door. (see interview transcript with Blodwen Bryan).

According to Joseph Jones, President of the Mineworkers Union writing in The Coal Scuttle (1936): " we have learned from history the pit life of a miner was hell under earth for a less than bare existence of a wage, and that the wives and mothers often went without themselves to keep their men fit and healthy for work."

All these facts have led me as a writer with an avid interest in 'anything historical' to use details of experience within *The Gresford Letters* (my terminology) and conversations with individuals connected with Gresford Colliery, to add pieces to the Jigsaw of the Gresford Disaster, knowing that there always will be unanswered questions and therefore missing pieces.

CHAPTER 2
History of the mining of coal in North-east Wales.

Coal has been worked in Britain since Roman times albeit on a small scale until the Industrial Revolution, and there are records of coal mining in North Wales from the fifteenth century, when mining rights were granted to leading local families, throughout Denbighshire and Flintshire by the Crown. The earliest form of mining was coal dug from the surface and the first type of mine was the Bell Pit where the coal was raised by hand from a shallow pit, later a horse-whimsey supplied the means of raising both miners and coal out of the ground.

From 1703, coal was used in lead-smelting and to fuel steam engines which were also used to pump water out of the mines. The market for North Wales coal was mainly a local one, the local pits were small and many with difficult geological problems, and by the late nineteenth century production had fallen well behind that of the South Wales coalfields which were 'ideally placed' to supply an export market. At one time there were literally hundreds of small pits in North Wales, some so small they were operated by one or two men; an examination of a nineteenth century map of the village of Rhosllanerchrugog gives a clear indication of the haphazard and widespread nature of these workings[4].

As coal output increased, a development that altered the course of coalmining in the North-east Wales coalfield was the ability to sink deeper shafts, thus providing extra employment for thousands of local men in this area. Two collieries with deeper shafts were Gresford and Llay Main. However, the sinking of these deeper shafts was not problem free, ventilation, haulage and winding and the men's exposure to explosive and poisonous gases were all major worries.

The advent of mechanisation brought extra problems, large quantities of dust were generated greatly increasing the risk of silicosis, a disease of the lungs rare in the pre-machine days, and nystagmus - damage to the eyes - said to be caused by straining to see in the dark through the dust. The machines eliminated the skillful part of the miner's work relegating him to what was felt to be an inferior position, but the machines were employed to the best advantage only when they were working at full capacity and without stopping; so the men had to keep pace and consequently there was an increased strain on them[5]. The increased hazards of working in the coal industry brought various regulations notably the COAL MINES ACT (see Appendix).

By the first quarter of this century very few of the smaller mines had survived, the larger ones were owned and operated by companies, who themselves had to battle against the "changing economics" of mining; Economic historians are divided as to whether management resistance to the mechanisation of coal cutting was a rational response to unfavourable geological conditions or a sign of technological backwardness and entrepreneurial failure.[6]

The main coalfield in the North-east Wales area was a narrow strip, only nine miles across at its widest point, extending from Oswestry on the Shropshire borders up to Point of Ayr on the North Wales coast. Gresford lies about halfway along the crescent of coal measures in the southern section of the coalfield, within the county of Denbighshire centred around Wrexham, (the largest industrial town in the area) Brymbo, Ruabon and Chirk and separated from the other coalfield in Flintshire by the Bala Fault, Gresford colliery on the outskirts of Gresford village consisted of two shafts, the Dennis and the Martin.

Plans to sink the shafts at Gresford were made by the United Westminster and Wrexham Collieries Ltd of which Mr. Henry Dennis was Chairman and Managing Director. When he died in 1906, he was succeeded by his son Henry Dyke Dennis. The Dennis shaft was sunk in the spring of 1908 and the Martin, some 65 metres away, the following year but complications of running sand and drainage problems meant that the sinking was not completed until March 1912. The two shafts, Dennis and Martin, went down some 680 metres before they met the faulted Main Seam, which was between two and three metres thick, the Dennis carried men and coal and took fresh air down, and the Martin carried men and supplies and brought stale air out, there should have been a third shaft, for extra ventilation and escape.[7]

When Gresford was opened it "absorbed" many workers from the smaller pits in the Wrexham area which were closing down. By 1914 there were 899 miners employed at Gresford, 689 of whom worked underground. By 1934 there were over 2200 miners of whom 1850 worked underground. The peak for British coal production was reached in 1913 with a total of 287 million tons. At that time there were 34 pits at work in the North Wales coalfields, mostly in Denbighshire where 14,500 men were employed producing 3.3 million tons.

The American Wall Street Crash, October 24th, 1929 heralded the start of the Depression worldwide, as thousands of investors were made bankrupt and the demand for goods of all types fell away. Men, were laid off and factories closed, overseas trade almost ceased and inevitably millions in industrialised countries were left unemployed. Despite abandoning its free trade to protect its industries Britain never regained its commercial foothold. The agreed reparation by Germany from the First World War of supplying coal to Britain, France, Belgium and Italy had already affected the export markets of the coal industry in South Wales and other coalfields in England.[8]

Unemployment (see tables in Appendix) was not the 'widespread' problem in the 1930's as is believed, it was confined to trades in certain areas; however in these areas, the people's lives were very badly affected. Coalmining was the third highest industry after iron and steel and shipbuilding, affected by unemployment, causing depression in the areas where there was a coalfield. The depressed areas had concentrated exclusively on the older industries such as coal, so that there was no alternative employment to be had, and since the majority of unemployed could not afford to move anywhere else they had to stay locally.

In 1931 the second Labour Government decided that instead of a programme of colliery closures as there should have been, every colliery would have a quota. When the quotas were given the collieries knew what they were allowed to produce, and in the case of Llay Main and Gresford Collieries, this meant that they had to sack some of their workforce, 600 men from Llay Main and 400 from Gresford.[9]

The collieries, like other Industry, had to work shorter hours and this meant that Gresford Colliery had to work a three day week. This had a profound effect on the miners and their families, causing them untold hardship and suffering, for a man had to work less than three days a week to qualify for unemployment payment. Ithel Kelly, the last acting manager at Gresford before its closure, recounted that his father, in 1934, was bringing home 14 shillings a week;

there were eleven of us children, ten shillings of that was the rent money, that had to be paid, I can't begin to tell you how hard it was for the families. The deprivation was enormous and although the conditions at

Gresford were extremely difficult, people would be reluctant to pack that up as there were no other jobs on offer anywhere. Unemployment stood at 41% in the Wrexham area, socially the majority of working people were a very deprived class.[10]

A contributory factor of this particular deprivation, was that the Gresford Colliery profits had to be shared by so many people, not only a share to the owners of the Colliery, the United Westminster and Wrexham Collieries Ltd, and the workers wages, but the owner of the land where the Colliery was sited, Lord Kenyon, had to be paid a royalty. The truth of it was that the person who owned the land owned the royalties on the coal.

Successive governments since the 1920's had looked at the 'royalties situation' to see if there was any way round it, but as so many people would have been affected there was no easy solution, that is, until the end of the War when the Coal Industry was nationalised. Another added expense, of having to pay royalties, which in turn affected the profits and so affected the workers, was having to pay rent for an area of land where there was coal to be worked, yet because of the quota system they could not work it at that moment in time, but had to take an option on it for future use. For example the Dennis section of the pit, which was mostly under Gresford village and beyond the church, would also have been accessible to Llay Main Colliery because they were working in adjoining areas on either side of Gresford church. This could have led to Lord Kenyon, who owned all this particular land, offering the rights to the Llay Main Colliery if Gresford had not paid the rent (Ithel: Kelly called this a 'dead rent') For this option on the land, which they had had since 1918, was approximately £3,000 a year. As Gresford Colliery owners were paying this 'dead rent' they would want the men to get into this area as soon as possible to start producing coal and maximise their holdings and profits.[11]

Unemployment in North Wales was structural rather than cyclical in its nature simply because its economy depended on industries, such as coal, that had little hope of recovery. However as the effects of the depression in the North-east coalfield was never as serious as in South Wales it was never designated a Special Area in the Development and Improvement Act of 1934, even though the Gresford Colliery Disaster of September 1934 left nearly 2000 men unemployed.[12]

When **Collieries of Denbighshire** (cited by many in the industry and in various essays from the Denbighshire Historical Society, as the authoritative text on the collieries of the area) by George Lerry (Editor of the Wrexham Leader for many years) was first published in 1946, prior to the nationalisation of the coal industry, there were fourteen collieries still working in the county. By the time of its reprint in 1968 only Gresford and Bersham remained. The last surviving colliery in the Flintshire field was the Point of Ayr.

Evidence relating to the Wrexham collieries and their workings has rapidly disappeared under housing and industrial estates and reclamation schemes. The detailed financial history and associated evidence of the Gresford Colliery has gone, memory and recollection aside, with the agreed destruction by the trustees of all its records when the protracted negotiations resulting from nationalisation had been concluded. Only a few balance sheets and statements to shareholders survive, still, quite clearly recording this anxious period for those associated with the coal industry at Gresford in the 1930's. Where the Dennis and Martin pit heads of the Gresford colliery once stood there was a depot for the firm of Laura Ashley, and there were plans to build a dry ski slope on the site surrounding and above the old Gresford Colliery site. All traces of many other local pits have vanished, including photographs and records, and even the spoil heaps are disappearing, the last evidence of the physical/geographical coal-mining heritage of the Wrexham area.

Images of the 1930's

The 1930's were imagined and documented as no other decade has ever been. The images were often heart-rending - wide-eyed children in ragged clothes, disconsolate groups of men shuffling around the streets in idleness, desperate women amidst the worn-out clutter of damp, bug-infested kitchens, the defiance of a Hunger March - and, in their human immediacy, made to seem so natural as to be absolutely real.[13]

Although in the lives of most men and women the central economic experiences of the age were cataclysmic culminating in the Great Slump of 1929-1933, economic growth during these decades did not cease. It merely slowed down.... (but) what was worst this time was that in this slump its fluctuation seemed to be genuinely system-endangering.
Each country had to protect its own economy against outside threats and it appeared that the world economy was visibly in major trouble.
To refer generically to 'the thirties' as the ' hungry thirties' is to propound this myth of 'the thirties' without considering the whole – that is, class,

20

economics, ideology, unemployment and their crucial relationship to each other, also that the lived experiences of the people within their society.

'The thirties' should not be considered a single text. The history of the decade and the images that spring to mind are those of crisis and political upheaval. 'The thirties', have been neatly framed by, the Wall Street Crash and the outbreak of the 2nd World War. The single adjective of 'hungry' in relation to the thirties, like 'roaring' (20's) and 'swinging' (60's) is part of the "process of myth making." There was said to have been 'mass' unemployment - but this was another myth perpetrated by the adjective 'mass'. There were large numbers of men unemployed, but only in 'depressed' areas where industry had been hard hit due to loss of trade highlighted by The Hunger Marches.

The images of the dole queues, the Jarrow Crusade, Moseley, the British Union of Fascists and the various political parties who came in and out of Government in this decade all add to our understanding of 'the thirties'. The generalisations and such 'dramatic rhetoric' (as below) used to describe 'the thirties' have been made without satisfactory supporting evidence;
Next to war, unemployment has been the most widespread, the most insidious, and the most corroding malady of our generation: it is the specific social disease of Western civilisation in our time.[14]

The Welsh Miner and Mining Disasters.

I first realised the cruel side of mining when I was ten. Going home from school one day, I saw a grisly procession of miners carrying home the body of one of their mates who had been killed at work. Like everyone else, I stopped and doffed my school cap to pay a silent tribute, and then I made myself look at the body as it was carried past. It was covered with some dirty sacking and I remember thinking: "It's like carrying a dead dog."[15]

Another myth perpetrated by images and words was that of the miner. Dirty face, flat capped, a lover of racing pigeons and greyhound racing, and in the case of the Welsh miner - he was staunch Chapel with a wonderful baritone or tenor voice and loved the game of rugby.

Collieries such as Gresford and Senghenydd are synonymous with the word disaster in Welsh as well as British Coalmining History. Accidents and injury were an accepted part/risk of life in the mining communities of both North and South Wales. While it was the large explosions that made the newspaper headlines these were not the major cause of death underground. Many more miners were killed by roof-falls as by explosions, but as they tended to kill one or two at a time they very rarely made the news.

According to Joseph Jones, President of the Mineworkers Federation, lives lost by explosions accounted for little more than 5% of the total death roll, whereas 90% were caused by falls of rock, accidents on the haulage or in the shaft, and mishaps in a variety of other places including the surface. The figures for Lancashire and North Wales in 1933 bear this out: there were 2 deaths from firedamp, 61 from roof falls, 22 from miscellaneous causes and 5 on the surface. In 1932, of over 800,000 men employed, 907 met with a fatal accident, in addition 130,000 men were seriously injured. There were more men killed and injured in the mines every year, Jones alleged 'in a comparison which at the time of his writing still had emotional significance for his readers' than the casualties of the Gallipoli Expeditionary Force. The Miners' Federation claimed that one man in every five was injured, an average of 450 injured and five killed every working day. Miners often cited piecework - (pay dependant upon the amount of coal produced) as a cause of accidents as it encouraged the men to flaunt safety regulations to earn a living[16]

There were many incidents in the Wrexham coalmining area and one of the earliest and best known is that which occurred at Pentrefron Colliery, Talwrn, Coedpoeth. On the 27th September 1819, the mine was flooded, and out of the 19 men working underground, three were trapped by the water. After eight days the bodies of two of the missing miners were recovered and all hopes of finding the third man alive were abandoned. Although efforts to recover his body were continued, a coffin was prepared for his burial. After twelve days, two miners who were working at the far end of the pit heard a voice calling out. They dug out some of the rubble and found John Evans, the missing third miner sitting in darkness some 120 yards below the surface. Although he was obviously very weak he was able to walk to safety unaided. He had managed to survive by climbing above the level of the water, eating his candles and drinking the water which dripped on him from above. "Rather than waste the coffin which had been prepared for him, John Evans took it home and used it as a cupboard."[17]

The disaster at Brynmally Colliery, Pentre Broughton was the most serious accident in the North-east Wales coalfield until the Gresford Disaster forty-five years later. On 13th March 1889, " just as the morning shift was about to surface, an explosion killed 20 men and boys, half a mile from the pit bottom." Six of the men killed were under fifteen years of age. When the bodies were finally recovered they found the evidence pointing to the cause of the explosion: - open lamps, matches, tobacco, pipes and lamp keys. "This complete disregard for standard safety regulations undoubtedly was the cause of the explosion."[18] Human blunders usually do more to shape history than human wickedness.[19]

At Ponciau, on 4th September 1894 a plank was dropped, accidentally, down a small pit and a man was overcome by gas in his effort to retrieve it. A fellow worker, Robert Evans was lowered into the pit and managed to tie the unconscious man to a rope, by which means he was pulled to safety. By the time the men brought Evans to the surface he was dead. Another similar accident happened at Ponciau during the miner's strike of 1926 when many miners sank small shafts in their gardens. A man was overcome by gas, and a second man died trying to rescue him.

Time and time again lives were lost in coal mines all over the world, repeating the same mistakes. At the Universal Pit in Senghenydd, Mid Glamorgan, South Wales, 439 lives were lost in 1913 and at the Gresford Pit in Denbighshire 266 lives were lost in 1934. (see list of disasters – in appendices). Although the loss of life was greater at Senghenydd it was the Gresford Disaster that caught the public's imagination, and gave the power to shock: For more than twenty years there had been a comforting belief, sustained by "official pronouncements", after the Inquiry at Senghenydd, that such avoidable accidents were a thing of the past, and that such a thing would never be allowed to happen again, but it did, and the same Inquiry took place in Wrexham twenty one years later, offering the same excuses, recommendations and regrets.[20]

Some mining disasters were unavoidable accidents for which no one could be blamed, but others such as Gresford were avoidable, therefore more tragic. No lessons were learned from the two previous explosions at Senghenydd, had this been so, the disaster at Gresford might never have happened. The 'Colliery Guardian'1934, pointed out that the average annual death rate from explosions had dropped from 0.65 per 1000 employed during the decade 1873-82, to 0.06 for the decade 1923-1932. This was of little or no consolation to the bereaved of Gresford.

In both editions of 'Come all ye Bold Miners'.[21] and 'Folk Song in England.' A.L. Lloyd included a ballad written about the mining disaster that occurred at Gresford, (see frontispiece) he said that all the songs he included meant much to the coal miners, and that a good song is one that ' Positively affects the community for whom it is destined, making for a clear reflection of circumstances, that aids understanding of common plight'. He wanted to include songs that when sung would lift a weight off the heart rather then as singing for singing's sake.

Some to show the mettle of a community clearer than a shelf of history books... Human history is work history, many of the songs that working men have evolved for their own use are valuable documents for understanding what has made men move and what will make them move again.

Many of these workers also came from a great singing tradition - secular, religious, or both, the music and singing therefore was an important part of their lives - "especially among the Welsh miners", who have a strong history of musical tradition. During the course of time the pit-disaster ballads tended to pass from more or less personal tragedies to communal dramas and then on to themes of class struggle. Lloyd saw the depiction of the injured and dead not as toys of fate, but as victims of greed and neglect and stressed the importance to tell the *truth about events, the more so if it is falsified by the masters and their press.* Such ballads do not work by revolutionary appeals for their aim is to arouse emotion against injustice, to strengthen the sense of solidarity, to move beyond lamentation over the workers' plight to burning protest against their oppressor.[22] The mining disaster ballads thus were designed to inspire the charity of the hearer to raise funds for those left in distress. (However there is no evidence to suggest that this was the case for the Gresford Colliery Disaster Ballad).

In 'One Hundred Songs of Toil'1974, Karl Dallas confessed that he always doubted the authenticity of The Gresford Disaster ballad. He felt that the violence of its condemnation of the owners' hypocrisy was the sort of thing he would have liked to believe miners could make up, but that it all sounded too pat. The popularity of the origin of a song and its reception, and/or the historiography of the piece on offer - its wording for instance, does not necessarily guarantee its authenticity.

CHAPTER 3
The Gresford Colliery Disaster.

A naked man who ran three miles along the deserted road to his home from the coal mine gave the first news of the mine disaster at Gresford colliery near Wrexham. His clothes had been torn from him by an underground explosion which had ripped up the pit rails for yards around and filled the galleries with rock. Fire spread like lightning through the dust-laden air and some 260 miners, most of them entombed in the Dennis Deep Main were burnt to death. Rescue parties, equipped with fire extinguishers and oxygen masks, endured heat which scorched the clothes on their backs and burnt the soles from their boots as they stumbled along the workings. Wooden pit props burst into flame as the fire spread so that with every explosion more and more rock fell. After forty hours all rescue parties had to be called up and the mine shaft sealed up. The pit ponies were the last living things to leave the shaft; some of them had never seen daylight before.[23]

The name of Gresford Colliery is perhaps, more than any other colliery in North Wales, better known in Britain and throughout the world, because in 1934, it was the scene of one of the worst mining disasters in British Coalmining history. 262 men and boys died as a consequence of the explosion, and three more men from the rescue brigade died in a subsequent failed rescue attempt, another life was lost three days later when a surface worker was killed by debris from a seal which blew off the pit head, bringing the death toll to 266. Thus making the coalmining disaster at Gresford second only to the disaster at Senghenydd, South Wales in 1913 where 439 lives were lost.

The details of this disaster and the circumstances leading up to it, and the stance taken by some, during the subsequent inquiry, emphasise how little things had changed in the years since the first inquiry into safety in the pits nearly a century earlier. (see Coal Mines Act 1850.) So few men at this colliery were members of the Union, one of the reasons for this was that Union dues had to be paid, but because of the economic and financial climate of the preceding years, many men could not afford this extra expense out of their wages and therefore the Union was unable to wield any power to press for changes in the men's working conditions.[24]
At the Court of Inquiry convened after the mining disaster at Gresford, attention was drawn to "innumerable breaches of the law and of

regulations laid down for the protection of those who worked in the mine...
(also the fact that) the behaviour of the inspectorate had been deplorable.[25]

Gresford was described as a fiery pit. The deeper the workings were, the greater the heat, as much as 86 - 92 degrees at less than a thousand yards into the workings, and certain areas such as the 14's were also prone to dangerous collections of gas.
It was 'red hot' for a fortnight before the explosion according to the men who worked there, and one miner, William Duckworth 'got himself a larger drinking bottle and two pair of football shorts to work in.' Another man used to take six pints of water with him each shift, drinking about half before he reached the coal face, one advantage being that because he had so much water inside him he needed to eat less.[26]

Compressed air cutters were used at the coalface and shots were fired to bring down the coal, which was in turn loaded on to a conveyor belt and transferred to tubs at the bottom of the Dennis Shaft, the machinery used caused a great deal of noise and dust as well as adding to the oppressive heat. Explosions can be caused by the ignition of explosive mixtures of firedamp and air, coal dust and air, or a combination of both. Firedamp is a gas given off by coal, ('damp' in this context is derived from the German 'Dampf' meaning fumes), consisting chiefly of carburetted hydrogen (methane), or marsh gas. If gas was discovered then the normal procedure should have been to improve ventilation, remove the men and add stone dust to sources of coal dust, thereby reducing and removing the constituents likely to cause an explosion.

According to other miners, D.M. Lansley, John Hughes and Alfred Tomlinson, the gas was a problem; 'One could smell the explosion coming a few years before it actually happened, and it was in everyone's mind.' John Hughes said that the gas made him feel heavy and drowsy, he didn't want to do anything when he came home. Another man who worked as a fitter at Gresford, R. E. Edwards, and who took part in the rescue work said; everyone who worked in the pit had the feeling that, some time, something serious was going to happen. The conditions down the pit and the heat on working coalfaces, were unbearable. But we all had our jobs to do, and no one seemed to grumble; they accepted it as normal conditions.[27]

D. R. Grenfell speaking in The House of Commons (after the disaster) described the working conditions of some of the men at Gresford, where men were working almost stark naked, their clogs with holes bored through the bottom to let the sweat run out, with a hundred shots a day fired on a face less than 200 yards wide. 'The air was thick with fumes, and dust from the blasting ..... a space 200 yards long and 100 yards wide above the wind road was full of inflammable gas and impenetrable for that reason.'[28]

The truth was that in 1934 Gresford Colliery was demoralized from the top downwards. John Harrop, the company secretary was dying. William Bonsall, the manager, was left in sole charge of the mine, without an agent with whom to discuss technical questions... Bonsall rarely visited the Dennis section due to preoccupation elsewhere... and the undermanager Andrew Williams, a man with thirty-eight years experience, including nine as a manager and agent, had only come to Gresford the previous January... This left the operation of the Dennis in the hands of the deputies, of whom five were employed at night, one for each face.[29]

The pressure for more coal then, outweighed the safety regulations; We know by the 'state' that the Dennis section of the pit was allowed to get into, meant that all they were doing was maintaining output at any cost and the result was that the roadways were deteriorating. They couldn't have repaired them anyway, because of the 'state' the main Martin Return had got into meant that it would not allow vehicles to pass.[30]

The Explosion

The first explosion at Gresford Colliery happened around 2 am, on Saturday 22nd September 1934, originating in the Dennis section of the pit, causing extensive damage with heavy loss of life, due to men illegally working double shifts to free themselves for the weekend to attend the Wrexham Carnival, or the football match between Wrexham and Tranmere Rovers. '*My Dad was supposed to be working but as they were going to Blackpool he had the night off*'. (Mrs Williams – (Blodwen Bryan's close friend.) Except for a few men working near the pit bottom and one deputy and five other men who managed to escape from the district, all the men who were employed in the Dennis section at the time lost their lives.

The Gresford Colliery hooter would have sounded, summoning the rescue parties and informing the public at large that there had been an accident at the Colliery. 'Knockers' were also sent out to individual members of the rescue brigade and to houses of men known to be working at the Colliery that night. Parry Davies, Captain of one of the rescue teams, was woken by some-one knocking hard on his front door, 'some knocking similar to that which happened at 4 a.m. on Friday, 11 December 1924, when an explosion occurred at Llay Main in the Two Yard Seam when nine men lost their lives.' The message he received was that all rescue men were needed at Gresford - " 300 men down the pit and only a few had been got out." In his report he mentioned all the things that were going through his head as he struggled to get dressed quickly. For the men trapped down the pit but also for his own family who were still in mourning for his five year old daughter who had died the previous week,

The tears were still wet on our cheeks, and sighs still issuing from our hearts. Surely my cross was already heavy enough. I had a load, and yet here was more. A call for help, and had the load been double, here was something which no one could refuse. My duty was pointed out to me quite clearly, and the home I was leaving must try to bear the burden and hope for the best.[31]

Others found out a different way

We were going to Liverpool that day, on the Saturday morning, and I didn't want him to go to work that night. But he would go, and he said " Well I'll have a few days off." We were going with our little girl. I had a little girl then. So anyway ... it was the postman.. that came to knock at the front door. And the first thing he said was, " there's been an explosion in Gresford,"... " Well I nearly went berserk." [32]

For Mrs Bryan the consequence of the disaster at Gresford was not only the loss of her husband but the loss of her only child of eighteen months who " died grieving for her daddy" a few weeks later;

Oh yes. He idolised the world, her. Idolised her. Well we lost him of course; she was crying all the time for her daddy. She only lived for seven weeks after. Seven weeks to the day.

Parry Davies met with other members of his rescue team at the Ambulance Room at Llay Main Colliery, where they were transported by lorry to Gresford. This was about 6 a.m., the first rescue team was already down and *"the scene was indescribable, crowds of men, women and children, grouped about in the Pit Yard waiting for news of their sons, husbands and fathers".*[33]

Many of the crowd were unfamiliar with the Pit Yard and had travelled miles to be there to wait with others for news and to be comforted by those who had come up from the pit. The six men who had escaped from the Dennis section informed the manager and the mines inspectors that they had seen a number of bodies in the section, but attempts to rescue the men were halted by the ferocity of the fire that broke out in the approaches to the Dennis section after the explosion and by the poisonous gasses produced by the combustion. There were no fire-fighting ranges or water provided in use at Gresford, which meant that the fire-fighting equipment was limited.

It was decided to call a meeting in the colliery manager's office with the people involved, the colliery manager, the underground manager and the Inspector of Mines. They agreed to try and make access to the North Main Return to take a sample of air which would indicate, if carbon monoxide was present, that nobody could possibly be alive in this section of the pit. Unfortunately for the rescue team, already underground when Parry Davies was called, they did not obey the law according to Mine Rescue. If the instructions had been given in writing, to the rescue team by the senior official on duty at this mine, then the instructions would have been clear and concise. As it was they were given instructions by word of mouth, by a very junior official named Harold Thomas who told this team to "Check the state of the airway." The instructions that he **should have given,** was for the team to **check the state of the ventilation in the** airway. [34]

The first rescue team was comprised of four men, not five as the law required. There were three men from Llay Main colliery and one from Gresford, to show them the way, because maps were not available relating to that section of the pit, as the law required. So four instead of five men in the team, attempted to go into the North Main Return about half past five on the Saturday morning. The law stated quite clearly that a team must not attempt to go through an airway less than two feet high and three feet wide, that was the minimum requirement for a team passing through with breathing apparatus. The first team found that they were unable to go through and so the Captain instructed his men to return to the surface.

Although the canary they had with them when they first got into the airway had immediately dropped dead in the bottom of the cage -signalling all the information they needed, that Carbon Monoxide was present and that nothing could possibly be alive, - because, the instructions had not been given clearly, they continued on to find out the state of the airway and not the state of the air that was in it. The Captain of the team should have signalled with the hooter that he had strapped to his chest, instead of moving about as he talked, a sign that maybe he had not been properly trained.[35]

The fourth man of the team was told to turn around and get out, he panicked, as did the man following him and both started to run. In their panic their nose clips came off, as the gas would have been affecting them by now and they died where they fell. The other man in the team who was with the Captain saw this, also panicked and started to run out of the airway. The Captain tried to restrain him and both their nose clips came off, the Captain was fortunate to be able to get his inhaling tube into his mouth and managed to struggle out into the fresh air where there were people waiting to help him, but the other man was overcome by the gas and also died where he fell.[36]

So the decision was taken to Stop All Rescue. They had lost three rescue men and knew then that no one could possibly be alive in there. Parry Davies' team was sent to help recover bodies including the three men who had just died, they managed to get two of them out and could see the light of the third man, but were instructed by the Inspector of Mines and the Gresford Manager that it was too risky to recover the body and so had to leave it where it was - a man name Jack Lewis, and the teams came out. Rescue work was suspended until they had decided on a policy, waiting for other teams and equipment to arrive from other parts of North Wales and Lancashire.
Thousands of fire extinguishers were taken down the pit and even those from small private cars throughout the district were requisitioned. Loads of charged chemical extinguishers were brought to the Colliery, and loads of empty cylinders were returned to the Monsanto Chemical Works at Cefn for refilling.[37]

The rescue teams continued to fight the fire throughout the Sunday without success, as there were more explosions taking place beyond the fire and they knew that it was extremely dangerous. When asked by the Miners' Representatives what the position was, they informed them that in their opinion " there were grave possibilities of a further explosion which would involve the lives of 200 more men who were then engaged in rescue operations."[38] Nevertheless they had to see for themselves. Owners, Mines Inspectors and Representatives of the men would have to agree before an order to withdraw the rescue teams could be taken. It was soon realised that any hope of survivors was in vain, "the sides of the road way were white-hot and it soon became obvious that the rescue attempt must be abandoned or more men would be hurt."
Eventually they decided that the only way to extinguish the fire was to exclude oxygen from it and so the decision was taken to do this, by sealing

off the pit. Sadly it meant that they would also be sealing in the body of the rescue man who had died on the Saturday morning. The men of the rescue teams had worked for some forty hours before this decision was taken by the mine's owners and the Mines Inspectorate led by Sir Henry Walker, and a notice was posted at the pit head at 7.45pm on Sunday 23rd September to inform the waiting crowds, that the Management were going to have to seal the pit and were therefore forced to abandon any further rescue attempts which could endanger more lives. On the following Tuesday a further explosion shattered the seal erected over the downcast shaft, even though it had been reinforced with sand and girders, killing a man who was working on the surface - and so the pit was resealed with the bodies of the miners left in the Dennis section. Only eleven bodies were recovered, and in each case the cause of death was given as poisoning by Carbon Monoxide. Nearly 2000 men became unemployed as a result of the closure of the colliery.

The Decision to Open the Pit.

When the pit was unsealed five months later in 1935, teams of salvage men with breathing apparatus, explored the devastation to see what had to be done to get the mine working again. The Management kept on saying that they would recover the bodies so that they would all have a decent burial, but 5,000 gallons of water a minute were flowing down from the pumps half way down the pit, which was also full of gas and the one question at the back of everyone's mind was - did the rescue man die as a result of faulty apparatus, if so, a team would have to use a tremendous amount of apparatus to be safe. If they were thinking about opening the pit they had better know the state of that apparatus that was left with the body, so it was decided to go back down the Martin Return and recover the body.[39]

Parry Davies from Llay Main Colliery was appointed the Captain for this task along with Tom Charlton, the new colliery manager who had replaced William Bonsall, Dr. Wallace the coal owners doctor, Dr. Fisher from the Safety in Mines Research and John Collinson the Inspector of Mines in charge of the rescue station at Wrexham. The heat was tremendous because there was no ventilation at all. Heat due to the depth of the pit, the warmth from the rock, the oxidation of coal and wood, things that take place underground all making the temperature higher, and when they reached the body it was in perfect condition.
Parry Davies said yes it was in perfect condition, that he had gone to school with the dead man and was able to recognise him immediately.

The body was without a 'glammer' (a mark) on it. This was after six months of being sealed up. There had been no oxygen you see, but the fact that they were there and the fact that their apparatus was leaking oxygen and carbon dioxide was enough to then set off a reaction.[40]

Parry Davies, conscious of the inexperience of this particular team, realised that there was no way they could carry the body out safely so he made the decision not to take the body, just his apparatus. But when four days later Parry Davies went back with his own team to recover the body, they found that within that short space of time it had started to decompose and it was unrecognisable. They wrapped it up in a brattice cloth (a Hessian type cloth they used underground to help with ventilation) and brought the body out of the pit. Then the decision was made, never to recover the bodies.
Because to subject the next of kin to viewing someone that they could not recognise, just the badness and the hazards of going through it, just wasn't on. So they decided never to do it, and left over 250 bodies in the pit that was their tomb.[41]

The Inquiry.

At the Inquiry it was shown that the owners were urging output at all cost and were putting increased pressure on the men, who had no choice but to comply, as in this area of high unemployment, the Gresford Colliery was the only hope of employment for miners;
It was useless to suggest that the men could make themselves offensive to the management by complaining of circumstances that were perfectly well known to the management before the complaints were made.[42]
According to Pollard.(1984)the reason why the miners had to put up with the working conditions at Gresford was that by the 1930's the morale of miners in Britain was rock bottom, " they were betrayed over and over again even by their own political party." Also the historical and cultural evidence of the time, it is argued (and subsequently denied) points towards the fact that Gresford was working a derivative of the nineteenth century 'chartermaster system.'

A 'charter,'or 'chartermaster' was any ordinary coalface worker who was answerable to the management for his particular coalface, along with the fireman. It was the men under him who did all the work, but he had the biggest paypacket 'just for being a yes-man'. The Gresford workforce of 1934 was 'an embittered and resentful one, receiving wide variations in pay.' In one area of the mine, the 14s, the men were being paid 22.5 per cent more per shift than those elsewhere in the Dennis; 'some of them, probably correctly, interpreted this as a bonus for keeping their mouths shut, and to 'prevent' their noses from smelling gas and their heads from feeling dizzy."[43]

Ithel Kelly refers to this as 'Authority without Responsibility', the colliery company delegated the authority for running the different districts underground to the workmen, but this resulted in an inability of the workmen themselves to share out fairly what could have been a reasonable wage. The charter-master would have the say in who was hired or fired, he might not work for three or four days but as it was his section, he had the money for it. Although the Colliery had a quota of coal, (see background History) if for some reason they were unable to reach their quota they were able to bring people back on a Friday night to work extra - anything to satisfy the profit margins. This was one of the reasons that on that Friday night in 1934 there were more people in Gresford than normal.[44]

In order to keep their jobs men were doing more than they should, especially those further up the chain of command. Necessary improvement plans for ventilation were axed in favour of 'more productive work'. To push the coalface onwards, the shot-firing was hurried, and even the gas, dispersed by compressed air, did not deter them in their quest for the acquisition of coal. Although, at the time these measures were within the law and not felt to be a danger, the fact that they were unable to establish the source of the gas should have signalled a problem elsewhere that warranted investigation. Three months before the explosion it is purported that a miner, Alfred Tomlinson was making his way to a coalface when he was asked by the deputy Harold Amos where he was going as he wanted him to fire two more boreholes, Tomlinson is supposed to have replied; 'If you fire them you'll blow us all up to hell',(see Gresford ballad.) Amos is reported to have had it fired anyway and later denied that the conversation took place.

At this time in the 1930's, unemployment, in the Wrexham district was 41%, the figures did not include women or young men under the age of eighteen, and here we had a further two thousand miners joining this number. Yet, although two hundred and sixty six men had lost their lives in the disaster, and an Inquiry had been announced, anybody who was wanted by the Company in the forthcoming Inquiry was found employment, "there was no shortage of titles, there were land-sale managers, assistant land-sale managers, watch-room assistants and deputies."

Classes were being held at the colliery and at the Mineworkers Institute in Wrexham. They were called Safety classes but were in effect - classes in how to give evidence to the Inquiry.[45] These lessons were being given by the Inspector of Mines, 'poacher turned gamekeeper', who was there to see that the law was complied with – teaching these people to give evidence, how to all say the same thing. Although the barrister for the owners, Hartley Shawcross, promised that there would be no victimisation of men giving evidence against the management, the men were afraid to speak out in case of not being able to find employment at Gresford Colliery when it reopened.

When the Inquiry got under way properly it was headed by the Chief Inspector of Mines with the aid of two assessors, one of who was President of the Mineworkers Federation, Joseph Jones. There were many recommendations made to get the pit reopened. For example they needed to retrain all the rescue teams they had in all the collieries in North Wales, with this in mind an Inspector of Mines, John Collinson was put in charge of the Mine Rescue Station at Wrexham and he was to see that all work carried out was done properly and that men were retrained correctly. All the while they were sampling continually the air with pipes through the seals, when they decided that the Carbon Monoxide readings and the oxygen levels were correct, they could remove the seals and open the pit. The Inquiry looked at all different kinds of things, it started off alright but gradually as the officials working the Dennis section of the pit gave evidence, they became more and more cocky and were intimidating the witnesses. In the end they had to have police present at the Inquiry to keep things in order.[46]

It was to become apparent at The Inquiry that a big 'cover up', was attempted by the Mine deputies. Because of the 'charter-master system' they felt that they would be held responsible for any accident or disaster, yet they spoke up for the management even when giving evidence. After the disaster, some of the deputies' daily reports were discovered in the pit, although fifty-one reports for 1934 were never found, they had either never been made, or had been destroyed (as was widely believed locally) - it seems that record-keeping was never a strong point at Gresford. The Inquiry heard that William Bonsall, the manager, told his assistant surveyor, William Cuffin, to stop the testing of the Dennis roads and faces for gas, despite the fact that this testing was a legal requirement, in June 1934, only three months before the disaster. Bonsall allegedly instructed Cuffin to fabricate some measurements for his notebook only days after the explosion, for he knew that he would be called to account for his actions.

The conclusions, reached at the inquiry, was that a spark from a telephone caused the explosion, the manager and deputies were fined a paltry sum. The cost of the fines amounted to less than 25 pence for each man that died. (The transcripts of this inquiry, runs into many volumes and give a full account of what took place including all the evidence given. The transcripts are held at the Flintshire Records Office and at Wrexham Library.)

A fund was set up for the widows, orphans and dependants, and money and other different kinds of donations were received on their behalf. The dependants were given a weekly allowance and could claim for other relief from this fund. However, very little extra provision was made for those men who became unemployed as a consequence of the disaster.

As at the Senghenydd Disaster over twenty years earlier, where the majority of miners were also entombed, the Gresford relatives have never been able to lay their men to rest..........

CHAPTER 4
The Gresford Colliery Disaster Relief Fund

The gloom cast over the district by the untimely death in pursuit of their perilous calling of so many men in the prime of life was felt everywhere. The 'mourners went about the streets' and on one memorable afternoon hundreds of them were together in the ancient Parish Church at Wrexham. Few who lived through this time are likely to forget it. Its heaviness was relieved by the spontaneous manner in which literally thousands of people sought to aid the widows, orphans and dependents who had been bereaved in such tragic and depressing circumstances.[47]

The records of the Gresford Colliery Disaster Relief Fund and the papers relating to it from the National Union of Mineworkers, are held at the Flintshire Records Office, Hawarden. The collection represents not only the details of the setting up and administration of the Relief Fund but the record of the enormous response, locally, nationally and internationally to a 'major industrial disaster.'(Chief Archivist, Paul Mason, Report.) Flintshire Records Office. 1986:
The disaster at Gresford Colliery in the early hours of Saturday morning, 22 September 1934, aroused a great deal of public sympathy for the 616 Gresford dependants - children, parents, widows and others. Immediately the news was heard people started to send messages of sympathy and money, the Mayor of Wrexham opened one of the first local funds which later merged with that of the Lord Lieutenant of Denbighshire.

Over 10,000 letters, from donors and sympathisers, are estimated to be amongst the papers deposited. There were donations from many town and district councils, business and social clubs, workingmen's clubs and friendly societies, labour and trade union branches, the British Legion, a number from mineworkers' unions and lodges, and several from miners' associations in other countries. A telegram from Moscow extended "fraternal condolence ... on behalf of 700,000 Soviet coalminers." Women's branches of the unions and other societies, contributed separately, in addition to their parties, and the Women's Institutes and Girl Guides also offered to help in what ever way they could.

There were also a number of letters from overseas, including Welsh societies from South Africa, Cymdeithas Cymry y Penrhyn (Cape Cambrian Society), and the Sons of England Patriotic and Benevolent

Society, Johannesburg, who numbered many Welshmen among them. In Canada, condolences were also sent from the St. David's Welsh Societies of Hamilton and Ottawa. The battalions serving in Gibraltar and the Consulado of Uruguay also sent their sympathies to the families and relatives.

The largest number of letters however were from individuals containing messages of sympathy, donations and offers of help; from working and unemployed men and women, many in financial need themselves, written in the only words they could express, 'from the heart'. This was not sentimental gush, this was the heartfelt anguish of others who identified with the consequences of this tragedy. One widow from Dorset with " only my old age penchion" and " 40 years of trouble myself with a family of 17 all delicate" sent her small contribution, another her "widow's mite". Many preferred to remain anonymous, sending donations of 6d, 2s. 6d, 5 bob, a 10 shilling note, a pound, a guinea, often just notes and coins, others using postal or money orders, a few using cheques.

Countless gifts and donations of clothing and food were sent; an Aberdeen Fish Merchant sent 200 boxes of kippered herrings and a fruit grower in Kent sent three tons of apples to be distributed to the needy. Others called for improvements in miners' working conditions and declared the debt of gratitude that was owing to the miner, for their toil to produce coal. A significant number of letters offered to adopt children left orphaned or fatherless, many came from ordinary families, childless couples, or from couples whose own children were grown. There were offers from orphanages and of apprenticeships and domestic service. Included in the files of letters were those from men (often older and widowers) asking for 'a good, respectable woman left widowed by the disaster' as a housekeeper (with a view to marriage).

The Fund itself

The initial Relief Fund opened by Herbert Hampson, the Mayor of Wrexham, was merged with the general appeal made by Sir R.W. Williams - Wynn, the Lord Lieutenant of Denbighshire which reached a total, with interest, of £275,974 14s 0d. An official Mansion House Fund, opened by the Acting Lord Mayor of London, Sir Louis Arthur Newton, Bart, reached a total of £291,196 11s 3d. An amalgamated total of over half a million pounds.[48]

Representatives of public authorities and others joined to form a local committee under the Chairmanship of Sir. R.W. Williams-Wynn to see that "immediate relief should be afforded to the dependants in need of it". The honorary secretaries, William Jones (The Clerk to the Peace) and R C. Roberts (The Clerk to the Lieutenancy), were assisted by a Ladies Committee who considered such matters as adoption and child welfare, and a number of voluntary workers.

Grants and Allowances

Every deserving case, was said to be carefully investigated by the Committee and grants and weekly allowances were paid 'so that distress could be alleviated at once'. Widows initially received a 20 shillings-(£1) weekly allowance, parents 10 shillings- (50pence), and (adult) daughters also 10 shillings. The two funds (the Denbighshire and the Mansion House) were amalgamated to form the Gresford Colliery Disaster Relief Fund (GCDRF) under the provisions of a trust deed (30 July 1935). The monies were invested in the names of the three trustees, the Lord Mayor of London, the Governor of the Bank of England and the Lord Lieutenant of Denbighshire, with details of the dependants provided in a schedule appended to the trust deed. The weekly allowances, which were listed, had been increased so that widows now received 27s.6d. and parents 20s. A Central Board was brought into force to control administration and advocate policy, and the actual local administration and distribution was carried out, by a permanent secretary and staff working under the direction of a local committee based at Wrexham.(see GCDRF Report in appendices).

In addition to assisting the dependants of those killed, immediately following the disaster, the Local Committee made grants to miners who, as a result of the disaster, were thrown temporarily out of work. The account books record, that in the beginning the weekly allowances for unemployment ranged from as little as 4d to 2s.6d, but eventually rose to 6s for single men and 10s each to married men, with an additional 'one-off' allowance for loss of tools left in the pit. Immediately after the pit closure the men were told that they would have a few months out of work, as it was, the pit did not re-open for production of coal until January 1936.

Provisions of the original scheme which aroused disquiet because they were held to penalise thrift or hedge the grants about with stipulations contrary to the fund, - were eliminated on the appointment and decision of

The Honorary Actuary. [49]
The Honorary Actuary made the following recommendations:-
1.   That the principal as well as the revenue of the Fund was to be used to meet the outgoings authorised by the Trust, and the intention was that the whole of the Fund and its income should be used up during the lifetime of the Beneficiaries, and that they should feel at the same time, that however long they may live and be dependent on the receipt of benefits, those benefits would be fully secured to them.
2.   That a number of the Widows were under the age of 30 years, and the operations of the Fund might extend over a period of seventy years or even longer.
3.   It might be a permissible course after a period of 50 years from the date of the disaster to purchase Annuities for the surviving beneficiaries to provide for them during the remainder of their lives. (This was the course of action taken in the 1980's).[50]

Amongst the men receiving allowances or grants were the members of the rescue teams, some who were injured in their attempt to rescue their fellow miners trapped underground. The Northampton Town Boot Manufacturers offered to replace the boots of the rescue parties damaged in the fires. [Unfortunately it seems they were unable to take up this generous offer due to no-one having the 'gumption' to write to the parties concerned, verifying sizes etc!]
A 'visitor' was employed by the Local Committee to visit the dependants and to check on their health and well being and to help financially if needed, The Visitor's Records 1935-45 indicate what sort of help was given and received. Assistance was available so that children of dependants could go onto higher education and the Report also show the scholarships which were granted, and the successes achieved by the students in their examinations. Boys were encouraged into apprenticeships for which allowances and equipment grants were allocated. The Fund also had a Medical Attendance Scheme for 407 widows and children, which "provided dentures, eyeglasses and treatment by Specialists".[51]

The 1986 report from Flintshire's Chief Archivist states that; "the individual claim files, over a 100 in number, provide details of the circumstances of each dependant - income, children, etc., and the various grants received. Details of age, dates and places of birth will make these files a useful source of demographic and social history in years to come"[52].

What they do not provide however is the full picture, the total record, of how people managed to exist when they did not claim. For instance, the Medical Scheme mentioned above accounts for 407 dependants out of 616, what happened to the other 209? The Fund and the long-term management of it, was to make sure that no dependant would be left in poverty. There were 166 widows, 241 children and 209 other dependants when the fund came into operation, only the widows were given a pension for life or until they remarried, 'when a suitable lump sum was granted at the Board's discretion'. Allowances to children finished at the age of sixteen for boys and eighteen for girls, the reason for this was that the board felt that by this age these children were old enough to find work and be paid enough to live on.

The Gresford Disaster Relief Fund was closed after the death of the last widow. Blodwen Bryan was 99 years old when she died – reunited with her beloved daughter Isobel in the Gresford Cemetery.

CHAPTER 5
Remembrance – Looking Back

I had the great good fortune to meet and record my conversations with Blodwen Bryan of Coedpoeth whose husband died in the Gresford Colliery Disaster. Blodwen was the only surviving widow at that time, and Ithel Kelly, the last underground manager of Gresford Colliery before its closure.

Blodwen Bryan (L) and her friend
Mrs Eirwen Williams in 1991

Ithel Kelly

Coversations with Blodwen Bryan - December 1996 and early January 1997

Beverley:	What was your name before you married?
Blodwen:	Wolmsley.
Beverley:	Did you come from around here?
Blod:	Yes, yes, oh yes.
Beverley:	You were born here then?
Blodwen:	I was born in the end house, in the end house, then I moved to the middle one, and then I moved here.
Beverley:	Was your husband a Welshman?
Blodwen:	Well yes. His parents were Welsh.
Beverley:	Nowadays they speak of Gresford as a Welsh mine but in 1934 they referred to it..............?
Blodwen:	Ah yes. Plas Power was a big pit too, a coal pit round here you know.
Beverley:	Plas Power belonged to the Fitzhughes' family didn't it?

Blodwen:	Yes, yes.
Beverley:	So have you lived here all your life.
Blodwen:	All my life.
Beverley:	And your husband too?
Blodwen:	And died here too. He was in Gresford wasn't he? And he was thirty eight years of age.
Beverley:	He was so young. Many of the miners who died were only young men.
Blodwen:	Mm, yes.
Beverley:	How did he get to work?
Blodwen:	There used to be buses running.
Beverley:	It would have been a long walk.
Blodwen:	It is, unless you had a bike y'know.
Beverley:	And that made it easier...........
Blodwen:	That made a difference, some went on their bicycles from 'ere.
Beverley:	It must be four or five miles.
Blodwen:	Oh yes, yes, all that. It's three miles to Wrexham from 'ere.
Beverley:	Did you work as well?
Blodwen:	No, no, I stayed home.
Beverley:	Too much to do I expect? (Blodwen: nods and laughs) Everyone forgets about all the jobs women ave to do in the home.
Blodwen:	Yes, yes they do. I was ten years before I had my little girl... and she was eighteen months old when she was taken away.
Beverley:	What was her name?
Blodwen:	Isobel.
Beverley:	A lovely name. Did you come from a large family?
Blodwen:	Pardon.
Beverley:	Did you have brothers and sisters?
Blodwen:	Only one brother. And he died not so long ago. His daughter comes up to see me …..from Telford.

Beverley:	I haven't really come prepared today to ask you questions. I just thought that we could have a chat and see what comes out of it.
Blodwen:	Well you don't know what happened. You don't. You can't picture it can you?
Beverley:	No, no, it's very difficult to imagine.
Blodwen:	You Can't picture it.
Beverley:	No, no. I've read the different stories about what happened, those written by miners who worked in Gresford and the newspaper reports. I've seen the photographs that were in the newspapers and the video they made, including the newsreel. There wasn't very much about the wives, mothers and families…
Blodwen:	The families, aye.
Beverley:	Well there were things written, but it only seemed to be in passing and I was curious, being a wife and mother myself. Your husband was only thirty eight when he was taken from you…?
Blodwen:	Yes… yes. Well he..,they wouldn't know anything about it. They wouldn't know anything about it, would they?
Beverley:	N…
Blodwen:	Nothing at all. It's been sixty-two years since the accident.
Beverley:	He'd have been one hundred by now.
Blodwen:	He would, but I'm ninety odd y'know.
Beverley:	And you look very well.
Blodwen:	I don't feel so well.
Beverley:	I suppose the cold doesn't help?
Blodwen:	No, no it doesn't. Makes my bones ache. I've got arthritis and er, what d'you call that thing for the heart?
Beverley:	Angina?
Blodwen:	Yes, that's it, angina.
Beverley:	Have you always had to 'see to' yourself?
Blodwen:	Yes… yes. I went to Lond…. Liverpool when I was fifteen.

43

Beverley:	Did you?
Blodwen:	Domestic service y'know... Nothing else for us.
Beverley:	I bet it was one of the hardest jobs ever?
Blodwen:	(Laughing) It was hard.
Beverley:	I once saw a film where the butler even had to iron a newspaper.
Blodwen:	Oh yes, that's right. There was a lot of things you had to do... I stayed in Liverpool for a year and a half and then I went to London.
Beverley:	To London?
Blodwen:	Aye to London. To Hampstead.
Beverley:	How did you get that job?
Blodwen:	Well somebody who knew me Mother and knew me, asked her if I would like to go. So I went... I went.
Beverley:	How did you meet you husband?
Blodwen:	Oh well he was ... I'd finished in London and come home you see, and he came in with my brother.
Beverley:	So, HE made sure that you stayed this time.
Blodwen:	Aye,aye.
Beverley:	Were your husband and daughter very close?
Blodwen:	Oh yes. He idolised the world, her. Idolised her. When we lost him of course, she was crying all the time for her daddy. She only lived for seven weeks after. Seven weeks to the day.
Beverley:	Do you think losing her daddy...?
Blodwen:	Oh yes. I think so... Made a lot of difference.
Beverley:	It's so sad when you lose anyone. It's difficult to understand how other mothers, losing their husbands and sons down the mine, coped. There was so many of you, not just here in Coedpoeth but in other places such as Llay and Wrexham, as well as Gresford.
Blodwen:	Oh everywhere, yes, everywhere. I've got a cousin down there too y'know.

Beverley:	Nowadays everyone would have got together, there would be help groups and...
Blodwen:	There was Nothing. Nothing.
Beverley:	I spoke to Mr Kelly, and he was telling me about the Fund, about all the money that was collected and how he was involved in dealing with the allowances for...
Blodwen:	They didn't give us much. We only had one pound seven and six.
Beverley:	Not much ..
Blodwen:	Aye. It's gone up over the years with in, in...
Beverley:	Inflation?
Blodwen:	Yes that's it, inflation.
Beverley:	Not a lot, for a man lost.
Blodwen:	No you're right. It doesn't bring back what you've lost.
Beverley:	Mr Kelly told me about a 'high class lady' who'd written to the mayor asking him to find her a girl, who'd lost her father in the mine, to be a maid. She then listed a number of things that the girl must not have wrong with her. She must not be deaf or stammer. She was to be able to read and write, properly. She must be clean and tidy and not have a squint. The lady appeared to want to help, but on her terms.
Blodwen:	They were very cruel, very cruel. That's not helping is it?
Beverley:	How people behaved and how they reacted is what interests me, trouble is knowing where to start.
Blodwen:	(Laughing) No, nor where to finish.
Beverley:	You're right of course. There is So much. Yet there will always be something to supersede it, like the Aberfan disaster for instance. It doesn't mean that we should forget though, does it?
Blodwen:	No, no. ... They covered it y'know, covered it.
Beverley:	Yes I have seen. Mr Kelly took me to where the pit heads had been, on an industrial estate. Have you been there?
Blodwen:	No, no...

Beverley:	It's on ...
Blodwen:	I didn't go to see the wheel either. I didn't like that.
Beverley:	Did you know that Mr Kelly lives next door to the wheel, in a bungalow? His two sons live on either side of him.
Blodwen:	There you are. No, I didn't know that.
Beverley:	All that's left at the pit head now are two concrete stones, I found that upsetting even though I didn't know anyone connected with the Gresford pit. I felt a sadness.
Blodwen:	It's because you're sensitive. Sensitive aren't you?
Beverley:	I suppose so. I won't forget how sad it made me feel.
Blodwen:	We won't forget. It's something we will never forget. Not what we've gone through. Beverley: Well you can't can you.
Blodwen:	You Can't forget.
Beverley:	No.
Blodwen:	It's with you day and night.
Beverley:	Yes.
Blodwen:	You might as well say it.
Beverley:	Mm.
Blodwen:	It's with you day and night. You'll never forget. Never.
Beverley:	It's ... Even though I didn't have anyone ... I FEEL ... I feel strongly about what happened. Not just for the men that died, but for you and others like you, who were left to ... cope. I want to write about it as a way of
Blodwen:	Relief.
Beverley:	Yes, I suppose so, but if I feel so strongly, how must other people feel who lost men down there? ... It must have been very difficult for some people to have spoken about how they felt. We're much more open about our feelings nowadays.
Blodwen:	But we're not all made the same are we?
Beverley:	Maybe it's just as well. I am cross when I read about how a widow with a lot of children would be considered a good

	catch for a man just because she received an allowance for herself and her children. A good catch, huh!
Blodwen:	(laughing) Oh yes, you would be cross.(Blodwen: thought my indignation was Hilarious!)
Beverley:	You didn't have much from the Fund did you?
Blodwen:	No, but they've looked after 'It' well mind you. We're still having some now.
Beverley:	Have you seen the mural at Gresford church?
Blodwen:	No.
Beverley:	Maybe I could take you.
Blodwen:	After Christmas. You've got plenty on your plate.
Beverley:	Am I holding you up now?
Blodwen:	No, no, I've got all day. I'm past worrying now. If you're not in the mood there's no use bothering.
Beverley:	It must have been a big thing for you to go away from home at fifteen.
Blodwen:	Aye, fifteen, yes. I went all by myself to Liverpool. I'd never been to Liverpool.
Beverley:	How did you get that job d'say?
Blodwen:	Oh I don't remember now ... I think it was through my Mother. I think it was. You know, these women talking together.
Beverley:	Was there a train or a bus?
Blodwen:	Yes a train.
Beverley:	To go to London must...
Blodwen:	Oh yes, I went to London and the housekeeper met me at Paddington.
Beverley:	After the accident did you work?
Blodwen:	No, well I had the little girl didn't I ? I had her for seven weeks after, so I didn't go out to work ... Some forgot them didn't they? Some got married.
Beverley:	Do you find that difficult to understand?

Blodwen:	Well we're all made different ... but we, we carry ours, our own don't we? We carry our own.
Beverley:	Some believe that when you marry it is for life, and didn't want anyone after their husbands died. Is that what you believe?
Blodwen:	Didn't appeal, didn't appeal, ... and perhaps we were silly y'know. We're lonely in our old age y'know, we're lonely.
Beverley:	Wasn't there any sort of, 'community spirit' in Coedpoeth, anywhere you could go to meet other people, other women?
Blodwen:	Well, no, it's only Chapel or Church?
Beverley:	Are you Chapel or Church?
Blodwen:	Chapel, Welsh Chapel, on top of Alun Road.
Beverley:	Did you go regularly?
Blodwen:	Oh yes, at least once a week, but Chapel's different now, you only go once a month, on an afternoon. I haven't been for weeks because I can't walk far. They come to visit now.
Beverley:	Did the chapel people rally round after the accident, did they come to visit?
Blodwen:	Yes, yes, they were very kind. Yes, yes, very kind.
Beverley:	I'll write my name and address down for you
Blodwen:	Well, you might come again, mightn't you?
Beverley:	Thank you, yes I would like to. Maybe I'll be better organised with questions next time.
Blodwen:	Oh you come any time, any old time as long as you takes me as you find me. It's nice to see you and have a chat. It's awkward isn't it, for you? It's such a long time ago that I can't remember as well as I might.
Beverley:	If I asked the right sort of questions I might jog your memory, and you'll think 'I should have told her that.'
Blodwen:	I dare say I shall remember lots after you have gone.
Beverley:	Is there a good or bad time to call?
Blodwen:	I've got lazy y'know, I don't get up so early anymore.
Beverley:	So after eleven, when you've lit your fire?

Blodwen:	Aye that's right.
Beverley:	Do you still do your own cooking?
Blodwen:	Yes, yes. I don't have anyone to do, 'cept for Archie next door, he gets the coal in.
Beverley:	Here's my address and phone number. Can you read my writing?
Blodwen:	I can only just see it, my sight's gone dreadful ... A friend of mine died sudden y'know (coughs) and it affected my eyes. When the son came to tell me she had passed away, ... she was here on the Friday and was dead on the Saturday. It seemed to strike me y'know and I haven't been right since.
Beverley:	'It' seems to affect people in different ways doesn't it?
Blodwen:	Yes, yes.
Beverley:	So I'll see you again soon?
Blodwen:	Yes, yes. Any old time,any old time. I'll see what I can remember.

The following conversation with Blodwen took place in early January 1997. Ithel Kelly had died suddenly just before the new year. There was a big funeral service for him at Gresford church on the 7th of January that year.

Beverley:	Was religion an important part of your life?
Blodwen:	Well I'm Chapel if that's what you mean.
Beverley:	Did you find that the people from Chapel were helpful to you after the accident?
Blodwen:	Pardon.
Beverley:	Were the people from Chapel supportive, did they help you?
Blodwen:	No,no, didn't bother.
Beverley:	Didn't they?
Blodwen:	No, didn't bother. (laughs). You want jam on it?
Beverley:	Better swipe that from the record. Ha. You mean to tell me that all those good miners were not regular chapelgoers either?

Blodwen: No, I don't think so. Well.. I don't know, didn't know them all did I either, but I don't think so. Usually they had to ask you, to go to Chapel.

Beverley: So you had to, manage on your own then?

Blodwen: Well yes, yes. Well me Mother was with me of course.

Beverley: I didn't know that.

Blodwen: Oh yes, me Mother was with me. She lived till she was eighty-two.

Beverley: Was your Father a miner?

Blodwen: Yes.

Beverley: At Gresford?

Blodwen: No, no.

Beverley: Nor your brother?

Blodwen: No. My Father died at Plas Power, before the accident, at the old colliery.

Beverley: Did he work underground?

Blodwen: Yes, oh yes.

Beverley: Where did your brother work?

Blodwen: He was at Marchwiel.

Beverley: So your Mother had lost both her husband and son-in-law within a few years of each other?

Blodwen: Yes, yes. Tragedy doesn't come alone. We've lost a lot of men in the colliery. An uncle and a nephew of mine died the same day,- Plas Power, buried in Coedpoeth cemetery, then my Father died after.

Beverley: When you lost your husband, how did they tell you that there had been an accident at Gresford?

Blodwen: We were going to Liverpool that day, on the Saturday morning, and I didn't want him to go to work that night. But he would go, and he said " Well I'll have a few days off." We were going with our little girl. I had a little girl then.So anyway ... it was the postman.. that came to knock at the front door.And the first thing he said was, " there's been an

50

explosion in Gresford,"... "Well I nearly went berserk."

Beverley:	I should think you did.
Blodwen:	It was the postman who told me .. first ... It was awful ... You can't describe it. You can't describe it. It was so terrible ... All the lifesavers went down - until they closed it of course.
Beverley:	I've read a letter from a lady called Margaret Capper asking if it was possible for the bodies to be got out of the mine, so that families could give them a Christian burial, her brother among them, but she seemed to have been fighting a brick wall.
Blodwen:	No,no. There was no way they could do it. It was impossible, they said. Impossible to get them out, to get them from there. They didn't have a chance of having him home. It was awful, awful ... His name's on the stone in the cemetery ... but ...
Beverley:	But he's not there.
Blodwen:	But he's not there ... Me Mother and my little girl are there, but my husband isn't, .. Only his name.
Beverley:	I suppose I have a fairy tale view of death, I believe that there is always something, of the person you loved about .. in the house, around you ...
Blodwen:	Well you never forget them, never. It's sixty-two years since it happened and it's as fresh today as it was then.
Beverley:	He was a very handsome man, your husband, from the photos I have seen.
Blodwen:	Oh yes, (laughs) not bad.
Beverley:	Did he have a good sense of humour?
Blodwen:	Oh yes, aye he was funny.
Beverley:	Was he good with your little girl?
Blodwen:	Oh yes. and she thought the world of him.
Beverley:	Did you go back to work after he/they died?
Blodwen:	Yes, to the munitions.

51

Beverley:	I bet that was hard work.
Blodwen:	(laughing) You don't know what hard work was.
Beverley:	No, not like that.
Blodwen:	Me Mother lived with me then and she went papering.
Beverley:	Papering?
Blodwen:	Papering - (shouts) DECORATING! (laughing that I didn't understand what 'papering' was.)
Beverley:	What did you have to do in the munitions factory?
Blodwen:	Pardon, oh, erm, what d'you call it, .making concrete.
Beverley:	Pardon.
Blodwen:	Oh, not concrete, y'know, the things they fire.
Beverley:	Bullets.
Blodwen:	Aye that's it, bullets. (Now we are both laughing).
Beverley:	Concrete, ha, what would you have them do with it, throw it at the Germans?
Blodwen:	Ooh, ooh, well you must excuse me, I AM ninety six, ... There's a good likeness of my husband in a photograph on the wall in the other room... A very good picture of him. Many a one would've taken it down and put it away somewhere.
Beverley:	Just because he's gone, doesn't mean he should be forgotten.
Blodwen:	No, no, I don't think you'll ever forget... Some of 'em have done and, of course married quite soon after... Yes, yes, that's their life isn't it?
Beverley:	I'd be interested to know why and, what sort of man, some of them remarried.Whether they knew them well, whether the men were local and miners too. It's not fair to assume that because they married soon after that they didn't really care for their first husbands.
Blodwen:	No, no, but I don't suppose they carried their love as far.
Beverley:	Some of the widows had a lot of children....
Blodwen:	Yes, yes. And the Relief has lasted well y'know. We had one

	pound seven and six and we had that for years.
Beverley:	That wouldn't buy very much would it?
Blodwen:	Well it didn't. No. People thought we had the world and all y'know.
Beverley:	Yes I know they did. I have read newspaper stories and read letters, such as one from a council in the south of England who wrote and said that they would not be setting up a relief fund in their area as they thought that the families should be paid out by ..
Blodwen:	The Colliery.
Beverley:	Yes and other funds, from unions and such like.
Blodwen:	The Colliery didn't bother about us did they? We had one pound seven and six for years. And one of the men who was on the committee lived across the road here, and he used to come sometimes with a cheque for one pound seven and six, sometimes a bit extra.
Beverley:	Didn't you ever claim for other things, like, the dentist or new glasses?
Blodwen:	No, no, I haven't bothered, never bothered, just took what was coming to me and that's it.
Beverley:	It was unfair that some were claiming, grabbing everything
Blodwen:	Oh yes. Grabbing everything and others didn't bother at all.
Beverley:	On the record sheets you have a very small entry, while other women had pages and pages of claims.
Blodwen:	Oh I never bothered, never.
Beverley:	I thought that you must have worked as you didn't claim any extras.
Blodwen:	Yes I did, I told you, at the munitions works, in Marchwiel.
Beverley:	How far was that?
Blodwen:	Oh a few miles from here.
Beverley:	Did you go by bus?
Blodwen:	Oh yes, a bus from Wrexham (laughs) A bus from Coedpoeth and a bus from Wrexham.
Beverley:	So you had to change?
Blodwen:	No,no. A bus took us to the works and brought us back again.

Beverley:	Did you ever keep a diary?
Blodwen:	No, No. I wasn't clever enough.
Beverley:	Mrs Williams's Dad worked at Gresford didn't he?
Blodwen:	Yes, yes, but he wasn't there that night. And if my husband had listened to me HE wouldn't have been there either... It's been a long time, sixty two years and I haven't found another man, but I was quite content. You had to make your own fun. My little girl only lived seven weeks after.
Beverley:	It must have been dreadful.
Blodwen:	(whispering) Never to be forgotten. You can't explain it. You don't know what it's for, do you? I'm not religious but I like to live a good clean life.
Beverley:	What do you believe in?
Blodwen:	Pardon.
Beverley:	What do you believe comes next, do you believe in Heaven?
Blodwen:	Oh yes, yes I do, And whatever comes. It's to be. I don't want to be cremated, no, no.
Beverley:	Why?
Blodwen:	I want to be with my little girl.
Beverley:	Don't you believe she has already gone to Heaven?
Blodwen:	She was only eighteen months old, she didn't have time to do anything else.
Beverley:	I wish someone could explain it?
Blodwen:	Well you'll have to get a "higher up" to tell you.(laughs) You can't come to me cos I don't know.
Beverley:	(laughing)Do you think you could come back and tell me?
Blodwen:	My time isn't long yet.
Beverley:	Oh no, you'll go when you are good and ready and not before. At least wait for your telegram from the Queen.
Blodwen:	What, another four years, oh no I won't, no. They all say, you'll have a telegram but I don't want it, I don't want it.
Beverley:	You're telling me you've had enough?
Blodwen:	Yes, yes. I'm starting to get a bit weary now. My sight's not

54

	good, and er, I dunno ... They've put oney on one side for us, for burial.
Beverley:	That's good of them then.
Blodwen:	Well I won't have it will I? Life hasn't been easy y'know. No it hasn't been easy.
Beverley:	Do they give you coal?
Blodwen:	Oh yes, but I was years before I applied for it, and I wouldn't have had it then but for a new lady who came next door. She came here one Sunday afternoon and she said "Will you answer a few questions for me?", I said, what do you want. She asked me my name, my age and different things, "Well" she said, "A policeman friend of mine has given me a form to fill in, for coal, and I thought of you straight away, and that's how I had it.
Beverley:	So, it was the same as it is now, if you didn't ask you didn't get, and if you didn't know...
Blodwen:	And I didn't know. Some of the people in Coedpoeth had had it you see, but they didn't say anything, no, they didn't say anything.
Beverley:	Like, knowing about applying to the Fund for spectacles and dental work?
Blodwen:	But I've never applied for anything like that. I saved up for it myself, I saved up. I don't believe in taking like that, ... perhaps I'm soft.
Beverley:	I did wonder about the coal.
Blodwen:	I had a load yesterday. Very nice coal too.

Transcript of a conversation with Ithel Kelly, the last acting manager of Gresford Colliery before its closure and a well respected authority on the Gresford Disaster, who was also a trustee of the Gresford Disaster Relief Fund.

23rd August 1996

Ithel: **1932**. If we can just talk about that for a moment. When the agent of the colliery retired in 1932, Thomas Henry (inaudible) they didn't employ another agent, instead the role of the agent was taken by a man called John Arthur Harrop who had been with the company since he was a boy. He wasn't a mining engineer. Never been trained as an engineer and

55

so this left the manager in a very difficult situation. He had nobody with whom he could confer on mining matters or who could advise him or back him up. Also in 1932 the underground manager of the pit, a man named Tom Hughes had suffered with ill health and his health was to be on and off for the next two years ((Ithels terminology). So it meant that the Dennis section of the pit was not supervised as it should have been. There wasn't an under manager to supervise it in place of Tom Hughes and in fact the deputies were self-certifying themselves if you like, they were imposing discipline on themselves, supposedly.

We know by the gradual 'state' that the Dennis section of the pit was allowed to get into, meant that all they were doing was maintaining output at any cost and the result was that the roadways were deteriorating. The couldn't have repaired them anyway, because of the state the main Martin return had got into meant that it would not allow vehicles to pass. So that was another of the factors. (contributory to the disaster.)

Beverley: Could you explain to me what these numbers mean 14's, 29's, 20's?

Ithel: They are just to identify the districts. At one time they'd call it say John Jones's working place etc but they had too many John Jones' so it was better, easier to give them numbers. After the initial explosion at 2 o'clock on the Saturday morning of 22nd September they had to look at the problem. Six men had come out of the Dennis section and they informed the manager and the mines inspectors that they'd seen a number of bodies in this section. Now they were trying to fight the fires, the rescue men and the workmen of the colliery, they were trying to put out a fire that they had got at in the main intake part of the Dennis section, but they had no (proper)fire-fighting equipment. There was no fire-fighting ranges or water provided in use at Gresford, so the fire-fighting equipment was virtually non-existent.

It was then decided that they had to call a meeting in the colliery managers office with the people involved - that is, the colliery manager, the underground manager and the Inspector of mines. They decided that what they had better do was to try and make access to the North Main Return, and if they could, take a sample of air from there and if it had carbon monoxide in it then they would know that nobody could possibly be still alive in this section of the pit.

Beverley: But they didn't taken the readings did they?

Opposite : A Skematic diagram of Gresford Colliery Underground

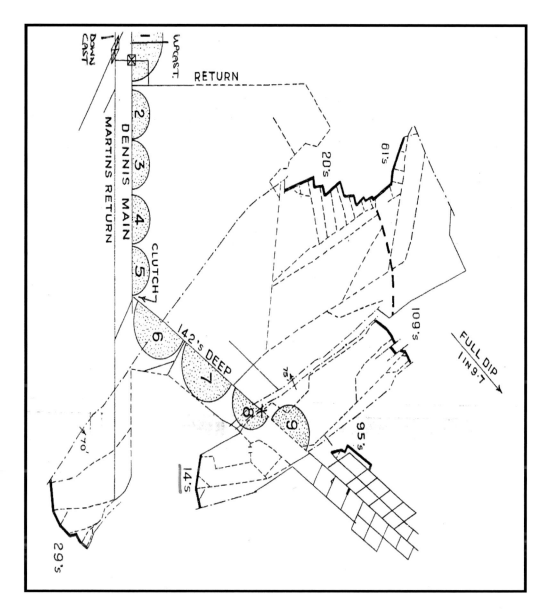

Ithel: No. They did not obey the law according to Mine Rescue. If the instructions had been given in writing to the rescue team, if they'd been given by the senior official on duty at this mine - that is the manager, then the instructions would have been concise. As it was they were given by word of mouth, by a very junior official named Harold Thomas who told this team " Check the state of the airway." What they **needed** to do was, **check the state of the ventilation in there.**

Now the team was comprised of four men, not five as the law required.(Mine Rescue law) There were three from Llay Main colliery and one from Gresford to show them the way, because they didn't have any

57

maps available, relating to that section of the pit, again, as the law required. So here we are, four men instead of five in the team, going into the North Main Return about half past five on the Saturday morning. The law states quite clearly that a team must not attempt to go through an airway less than two feet high and three feet wide. That was the **minimum** requirement for a team passing through with breathing apparatus.

The team went to parts of the North Main Return, where they found that they couldn't go through and the Captain signalled to retire - well in fact, he was talking to them. Although they had had a canary with them when they first got into the airway the canary immediately dropped dead in the bottom of the cage - now, that was all the information they needed. Carbon Monoxide was present, nothing could possibly be alive, but because the instructions hadn't been given clearly they went to find out the state of the airway and not the air that was in it. The Captain of the team, instead of signalling with the hooter that he had strapped to his chest, was moving about as he talked, that was because he had been badly trained. The Superintendent of the Mine Rescue Station was not himself, a qualified instructor.

The fourth man of the team, on that fateful Saturday morning, was given the message to turn around and get out. No why's or anything like that, so he panicked and started to rush and the man who was following him also panicked and started to rush. Their nose clips came off, as they would have been falling by then, and they died there and then. The third man in the team who was with the Captain sees this, panics and starts to rush out of the airway. The Captain tried to restrain him and both their nose clips came off. Fortunately the Captain was able to get his inhaling tube into his mouth and managed to struggle out into the fresh air where there were people waiting to help him.

So the decision was taken to Stop All Rescue. They had lost three rescue men. They knew then that they weren't fighting to save any life at all - nobody could possibly be alive in there. Other rescue teams were then sent to recover the three bodies of the men that had just died. They managed to get two of them out - they could see the light of the third man, but decided that it was too risky to recover it and would leave it where it was. So left it where it was - a man name Jack Lewis, and the teams came out. Rescue work was then suspended until they had decided on a policy. *(There had not been a disaster of such magnitude since Senghenydd in 1913, which everyone at the time said should never be allowed to happen again.*

They continued to fight the fire throughout the Sunday with not much success as there were more explosions taking place beyond the fire and they knew that it was very, very precarious.

On the Saturday night the man who had been acting as the mine agent between the manager and the board of directors, John Arthur Harrop, died. This left the manager in an awful position - who was left to take his part. The board of directors could say what they wanted. He was one on his own against them. If they were to say to him ' Well, what's gone on?' and he said 'Well I told Mr Harrop.' They could say ' Well I'm sorry old boy, he's dead.'

Beverley: Did he die of his illness?

Ithel: He died of his illness without knowing that there had been a disaster at Gresford. He wasn't a young man - a fellow of the Wesleyan cause and all that. Eventually they decided that the only way to get the fire out was to exclude oxygen from it. So, they'd recovered six bodies, making a total of nine altogether, now the decision was made to seal the pit off, exclude the oxygen and hopefully the fire would go out, but it meant that they would also be sealing in the body of the rescue man who had died on the Saturday morning. A letter was posted at the pit head at 7.45pm on Sunday 23rd September to say that they were going to seal the pit. On the following Tuesday one of the seals blew off. They had reinforced it with sand and girders and more sand but it still blew off and killed a man who was working on the surface - his death brought the total dead to two hundred and sixty six.

Beverley: How would they have told people that there had been an explosion?
Ithel: There was a hooter. A hooter would go summoning the rescue parties and informing the public at large.
Beverley: What about the people who lived in other villages?
Ithel: They would have heard the Gresford hooter.
Beverley: So nobody would be told individually about an explosion?
Ithel: Well the hooter would go and the knockers up would be going round. They used to have knockers up in those days - not everyone had an alarm clock.   Knocking your door, your window, your drain pipe, (anything to get you out on time for work). The knockers would go around informing people as soon as they knew. In time the Government announced that an Inquiry would take place into the cause and effects of the explosion at Gresford colliery. At this time in the 1930's you were looking at 41% unemployment, they didn't include women in these statistics or young men under the age of eighteen. So when you were told that unemployment was 41% this was horrendous, and here we were with

a further two thousand miners joining the dole queues. Well, not quite. Although two hundred and sixty six men had lost their lives in the disaster, and an Inquiry had been announced, anybody who was wanted by the Company in the forthcoming Inquiry were found employment, there was no "shortage of titles." (Ithel's terminology.) There were land-sale managers, assistant land-sale managers, watch-room assistants and deputies......

Classes were being held at the colliery and at the Mineworkers Institute in Wrexham. They were called Safety classes but were in effect - classes in how to give evidence to the Inquiry. These lessons were being given by the Inspector of Mines,' poacher turned gamekeeper', who were there to see that the law was complied with - teaching these people to give evidence, how to all say the same thing. When the Inquiry got under way properly it was headed by the Chief Inspector of Mines with the aid of two assessors, one of who was President of the Mineworkers Federation, Joseph Jones. With the Inquiry underway all sorts of things were to happen to get the pit reopened. For example they needed to retrain all the rescue teams they had in all the collieries in North Wales, with this in mind an Inspector of Mines, John Collinson was put in charge of the Mine Rescue Station at Wrexham and he was to see that all work carried out was done properly and that men were retrained correctly. They were sampling continually, they had pipes through the seals so that they could sample the air. When they decided that the Carbon Monoxide readings and the oxygen levels were correct, they could remove the seals and open the pit.

The Inquiry looked at all different kinds of things. When you go through the Inquiry you will see that it started off alright - quite civilised as a matter of fact - but gradually as the officials working the Dennis section of the pit gave evidence, they became more and more cocky and were intimidating the witnesses. In the end they had to have police present at the Inquiry to keep things in order.
There were two important changes I forgot to mention. In April 1934 a new underground manager was appointed to replace Tom Hughes, his name was Andrew Williams. Again, he had no time to be organised, he had to maintain output at all cost. He couldn't put right the things he wanted to because it would have meant taking men of production.

Beverley: Did they have a union?
Ithel:They **had** a union. The union agent for North Wales, a chap called

Edward Hughes, was quite old then, he'd been in the post since 1910. He wanted to retire and did so and a new Miners Agent was brought into office in January 1934, his name was Edward Jones. He was probably one of the most respected men in mining circles in North Wales, and went on to become president of the World Miners Federation.

But what of the unions? What did the Union have to say about these conditions at Gresford?

Less than 40% of the men who worked at Gresford were members of the Union. It was voluntary, you needed to go and pay it once a week, it was 4d. And 4d when you usually worked a three day week amounted to a large sum. The Union itself had no clout, even as late as the 1960's I can recall this. The Union always had the right to carry out inspections and to make reports about those inspections - one copy to the manager, one to the Inspector of Mines and a copy for their own records. Now they hadn't used that right, exercised that right, since the 1920's. One of the reasons for this was that if they were going to give a derogatory report, they would be told either to put it right themselves, or it would be put right, but it would mean that the miners would be on lower wages until such time as the work was carried out - so they were intimidated, they were in the 1960's and we had been nationalised since 1947.

This sort of thing definitely did go on, there was a reluctance to report this sort of thing. I know because I later went on to be the last manager at Gresford. I was manager at Gresford when they shut it in the 80's.

Beverley: Was it a sad day?

Ithel: **No, it wasn't a sad day, it was the best thing that ever happened.**

So these were the two important changes in personnel, a new underground manager and a new agent for the Union.

The Inquiry went on for 46,000 questions and answers. They were three weeks in Wrexham full time at the Church House and then they moved to the ballroom at the Wynstay Hotel and they went from there to the Institute of Mechanical Engineers at Ewloe.

You can go through the evidence. I have been through it many many times. You can go through it time and again and find something new and different, something that will jog your memory, something(s) you know are impossible and you will be able to spot where lies are being told.

Prosecuting on behalf of the workmen (miners) was Sir Stafford Cripps, a brilliant chap. He had given lectures to the Royal Society when he was twenty seven, a wealthy man who lost his father, was quite young. Representing the owners was Mr A T Miller. K.C. After the Inquiry had been going on for eight days the owners, United Westminster Colliery Company realised that their man was no match for Stafford Cripps 'so they changed their brief'. They got a new practising barrister in from Liverpool, R. T. Shawcross, he came in and took over the case. He was a tough adversary. As a result of what he saw and heard concerning the Gresford Disaster he became a socialist as a matter of fact. He prosecuted for the Labour Government at the Nuremburg Tribunal

If we look at this section where (it) started, in the 14's. The manager was asked in evidence relating to the 14's, how much air was circulated through the 14's district. He said 3250 cubic feet of air a minute, and the law required that readings were taken weekly. So he said 3250 cubic feet of air a minute and no gas was found, nor ever did. Now, in the 1950's we were working a coalface within 100 yards of the 14's, so the same conditions exactly, and the same length, 200 yards long in a seven foot six containment area, exactly the same. One difference was that we were drilling holes to capture methane and piping it to the surface. In fact it was being sucked out by big pumps, on the surface, sucking the methane from the coal area before we went in, so it would be safer.
We were 786 yards deep. We were circulating **37,000** cubic feet of air a minute and we **couldn't** comply with the law. We **couldn't** keep it **gas free**.

So that tells you that when they said that they **never** found gas and they were circulating one tenth of the air that we were, that somebody somewhere was telling lies. Similarly the deputy who was in charge of the 20's section was asked about the state of the return airway where the rescue man died. He said that it was in excellent condition and that you could walk upright. The rescue party had said that it was **two feet** high. So when they had all been taught to give evidence, 'they'd all been told to sing off the same hymn sheet' - the answers were coming off pat.

Stafford Cripps realised this and when he was questioning the 20's district fireman and official in charge, Richard Owen he said 'Tell me, your district stretches from 20's back to the Martin?'
'Yes.'
'What sort of condition was it in?'

'Oh, good.'

'What sort of ventilation did it pass?'

He rolled all the figures off pat, '10,000 cubic feet of air a minute,' then he asked him (Owen) further questions to get him feeling in a nice and secure frame of mind, then Cripps asked him what time did he start the inspection on the end of an afternoon shift and was told about 6 o'clock. Then Cripps asked him what time would he reach the Martin and was told about half past seven

'What you are saying is, to travel less than one mile was taking you an hour and a half. Either you are a very slow walker or conditions were difficult, and if the roadways were as good as you say why did it take you so long?'

'Oh I probably did it quicker than that.'

'No, no, your first answer was the correct one. You were part crawling because of the state of that roadway.'

Things like that came out continually. We know now from the amount of coal that was produced then, what roughly the level of gas was. So on and so forth, we were able to get a true picture of the horrendous conditions there were in the Dennis. They kept on saying that they would recover the bodies and they would all have a decent burial. Well that was alright except, once the seals on the pit were removed....

Erm, well you could talk for a day about the job of reopening the two shafts themselves, on the science involved, as it was such a tricky, tricky business going down into a pit where you needn't go. 5,000 gallons of water a minute were flowing down from the pumps that were half way down the pit. The pits were full of gas and the one question at the back of everyone's mind was - did the rescue man die as a result of faulty apparatus, if so, a team would have to use a tremendous amount of apparatus to be safe. So if they were thinking about opening the pit they'd better know the state of that apparatus that was left with the body. The best thing to do would be to go back down the Martin return and recover the body. They had been sealed up for six months.

They appointed one of the rescue men at the colliery as Captain, a man named Parry Davies who worked at Llay Main. With Tom Charlton, the new colliery manager who had replaced William Bonsall, Dr. Wallace the coal owners doctor, Dr. Fisher from the Safety in Mines Research and John Collinson the Inspector of Mines in charge of the rescue station at Wrexham. Parry Davies led these men to recover the body.

The heat was tremendous because there was no ventilation at all. Heat due to the depth of the pit, the warmth from the rock, the oxidation of coal and wood, things that take place underground all making the temperature higher, and when they reached the body it was in perfect condition.

 Parry Davies said yes it was in perfect condition, that he had gone to school with the dead man and was able to recognise him immediately. The body was without a 'glammer' (mark?) on it. This was after six months of being sealed up. (There had been no oxygen you see, but the fact that they were there and the fact that their apparatus was leaking oxygen and carbon dioxide was enough to set off a reaction.)

Now when Parry Davies saw the state of this team he realised that there was no way they could carry the body out and he made the decision not to take the body, but just his apparatus. They would have to recover the body at a later stage. But when four days later Parry Davies went back with his own team to recover the body, they found that it was unrecognisable, within that short space of time it had started to decompose. They wrapped it up in a brattice cloth (a Hessian type cloth they used underground to help with ventilation) and brought the body out of the pit. Then the decision was made, **but never publicised**, never to recover the bodies, because to subject the next of kin to viewing someone that they couldn't recognise, just the badness and the hazards of going through it, just wasn't on. So they decided never to do it, and left over 250 bodies in the pit that was their tomb. In the meantime the Mayor of Wrexham had started a Fund. Now I am one of the trustees of the Disaster Relief Fund, over £560,000 was invested from the collections made. There were 546 dependents when this was started and the youngest widow was 14 years of age.

Here Ithel reads me a letter sent to the committee from a woman in Wembley requesting help in finding a suitable girl to help. I refer in detail to this particular letter later in this book because the woman takes great pains to list what attributes the girl must have and what disabilities she must NOT have! Ithel also made mention here of the many orphanages and hotels and boarding houses who wrote offering holidays or places AT REDUCED RATES, obviously hoping to cash in on the money available from the Fund.
Ithel: The Lord Mayor of London was the Chairman of the main fund, the Lord Lieutenant of Denbighshire was Chairman of the local fund and everyone else acted on an honorary basis. The committee had an Inspector to go around to see that the money was being used properly, because, remember a miner working at Gresford was on a three day week due to the quota system which had been brought in by the Labour Government, the short lived Labour Government of the 1930's. So employment was very

spasmodic, miners were only getting 7s 9d a day, less than £1.4s a week, also by virtue of working three days they were unable to claim dole money. If you had a widow who had an income for herself of £1.7.6d and an allowance for each child she would prove something of a good catch,' if you could get your feet under the table there.' Some of these widows had a number of children so would be receiving well over £2 a week, depending on their circumstances and more if they claimed for all the things they were allowed to claim for, holidays, convalescences, mourning money and medical expenses.

The people who drew up the trust deed for the Gresford Disaster were so far seeing, there is still some money left in other colliery funds that no one can touch and all the dependents are long gone. The people who drew up the deed gave their services for free, bank managers, teachers, professional people who night after night spent hours opening and replying to letters. They drew up this deed in such a way that when the last dependent died there would be no money left in the fund, the last penny would be spent but the fund would have seen them out. The committees had to consider the lifestyles of the dependents, all sorts of other possibilities, even to the extent in calculating how long they would live. The money had to be administered according to this trust, they did a brilliant job and we have stuck by it ever since.

When the Company opened the pit and wanted workmen back and, although an undertaking had been given by Hartley Shawcross (the owners barrister) that there would be no victimisation or discrimination against anyone who had given evidence on behalf of the men, in fact there was.
I know of men who went to the colliery to look for a job, when people were starting to be taken on when the pit was being redeveloped, who were told that there were no vacancies as they'd taken on their quota of men, closed the shutter of the window and waited until the man/men were out of sight, reopened the window and start signing on again. In 1961 I was the assistant underground manager then, it was a time when you could sign on labour if they came looking for a job, and I was there on the Saturday morning and a man came looking for a job, his name was J. R., first class chap. I was interviewing him finding out what he knew about the pit and looking at his hands to see if he was a worker or whether he had 'piano fingers', you soon know who you were talking to.
In the course of the interview there was a knock at the door and a man employed there, whose Father had worked at the mine at the time of the disaster asked if he could have a word with me. I said, "I'll see you later

on", he said it was rather urgent and so I went into the corridor to speak to him and asked what he wanted. He said "Is that man looking for a job?" and I said that he was. "Oh you shouldn't give him a job Mr Kelly he gave evidence against us at the Inquiry."

This was in 1961, twenty six years since the Inquiry. I told him to clear off. Not in those words but in words that he would understand and would take on and I went back and signed up J.R. By then he was a man in his fifties, his brother was one of the victims in the pit, and a bandsman. To try and deny a man work, well, anyway I signed him up and he turned out to be an excellent chap. If that was an example of what the attitude was like in 1961 just imagine what it was in 1935. Certainly it was a maddening situation.

Beverley: How did those men who had given evidence for the owners continue to live and work and the area?

Ithel: Well the owners were in a very, very strong position. They could blacklist you from every pit in North Wales. So it kept you in line. You learned very quickly who would get all the best shots. You had to bite your tongue or else, if you couldn't control it then you paid for it, no question about it. This was why, when 1947 came and there was nationalisation in the pits quite a number of people left - they knew it was the day of reckoning. The day when they could throw their weight around, because they were the managers' men if you like, company men was the term used, was well and truly over. I'm talking about five years before I joined the management so I know what it was like from both sides, the worker and the management.

Beverley: Did the Duke of Westminster, as a shareholder, do anything to help?

Ithel: No, no, he didn't get involved on a personal basis, he invested his capital, and invested wisely. A lot of people like him got out when the Royalties Act came in. The royalties applying to the collieries was that if you took coal from under somebody's land you had to pay them so much for each ton extracted, some of them didn't even know the colour of coal. This meant that vast landowners, the Duke of Westminster was one of them, were earning thousands of pounds by virtue of others taking coal from his land, he wouldn't even know it was gone.

He had agents working for him, looking after his interests, the Church commissioners were another body who owned tremendous amounts of land so benefited from coal being mined. They even sent their own people down the pit to conduct their own surveys to make sure you were where you should be working.

Beverley: How did the men clock on for work?

Ithel: With the tally system, but Gresford didn't have a 'checking' system such as was required by the 1909 Act, there was a lamp check but it wasn't a personal check. On the Saturday morning (of the explosion) at 9 o'clock they thought that they were talking about 100 to 120 men, on Sunday morning they still didn't know how many men were missing and it was only on the Monday afternoon that they found how many men were buried in the Dennis section of the pit.

Beverley: Could someone have gone down the pit and not been accounted for?

Ithel: It was very unlikely and I'll tell you why. When you drew your lamp and tally you would walk across to the 'circus' put your tally in a tin and then you would go down the pit. Once you went to your district, whether it was the 20's, 29's or 14's there would be a fireman there with a book. He'd got your name down as working in that district so he'd either be able to put a tick or a cross by your name. You'd make sure that you had a tick by your name, as that's why you came out to work (to get paid.) At the end of the shift he would take his book to the time office and the names would have been recorded onto the master sheet

Beverley: So did the book tally up with the tallies in the tin?

Ithel: No (only the numbers) because the tallies were not used as a check, just for a body not a name. You could have a different lamp everyday, for they never had the tallies tied to a name, they weren't a personal thing. That was one of the anomalies it would have been so easy to tie a lamp and a tally to a number so that you would know who was who but that didn't happen; and because they didn't know it meant that they had to go knocking to see which men had been working (and were now thought to be dead.
Beverley: How did the men get to the pit?

Ithel: On a bike, by bus or on a lorry covered over with tarpaulin.
Here Ithel starts to tell me about Blodwen (who he had got to know when he became a trustee and a visitor for the Relief Fund) as he knew of my interest in Coedpoeth and told me that there had been a lorry for

67

the men from Coedpoeth to the pit. He told me about how Blodwen had lost her daughter Isobel shortly after losing her husband and the fact that she never remarried, which then led onto the following information about other women who he had obviously got to know of because of his involvement and interest in the Explosion and the Relief Fund.

Ithel: Once, whilst visiting Mrs Williams (one of the three widows left alive in 1995) she told me about one of the dependants, a girl named Gladys Pugh. This girl was the daughter of Mrs Williams's sister who had died three years before the disaster. Arthur Pugh,(the father) and Gladys went to live with Mrs Williams and after the disaster, Mrs Williams became the guardian of Gladys who attended Rhosrobin school until she was 14 years of age. On leaving school she was employed in a shop, Brown's Wine Merchants in Wrexham for a wage of five shillings a week but had to work from 9 o'clock in the morning till 9 o'clock at night six days a week. These long hours affected her health and she was forced to leave.

She was then unemployed until November 17th 1938 when she obtained a job as a nursemaid in West Kirby receiving 6s 6d a week and her keep. After being there for two weeks she came home on her day off and found that Mrs Williams and her child had Scarlet Fever. When she returned to her situation at work she informed her mistress of this fact and she immediately dispensed with her services.

Another girl, a seventeen year old orphan, was discovered by a visitor working at a fish and chip shop for no wages, in addition she paid 10 shillings from her pension from the Fund for her keep. (She was entitled to money from the Fund, as a pension, until she reached the age of eighteen.) She complained to Mr Jones, the visitor, that the work was hard and the hours were long. This was in March 1939, she was advised to go to the Registry in Wrexham to get a job in Service as the allowance she was receiving from the Fund would shortly cease now that she was coming up to eighteen, also the compensation of £2 a month that she was receiving from the holding stock would also cease. In May 1939 she was still working in the fish and chip shop for which she was now being paid 2s 6d and her keep. Mr Jones the visitor reported these facts and felt that advantage had been taken of this girl and his recommendation was that she should go into Service where she could earn at least 10 to 12 shillings a week. (There were no more entries under her name - presumably because when she reached eighteen she was on her own.)

The following extract is taken from a conversation I had with Ithel a few months later.

Ithel: 1931. In 1931 we had the second Labour Government and instead of a programme of colliery closures as there should have been they gave every colliery a quota. When the quotas were given they knew what they could produce, and in the case of Llay Main, they sacked 600 men. Gresford also had to sack over 400 men. The pits, like Industry, were going on short time and Gresford went on a three day week. If you worked less than three days you qualified for unemployment, so you can imagine this had an effect on the families and times were extremely difficult. My father at that time was bringing home 14 shillings, there were eleven of us children, ten shillings of that was the rent money, that had to be paid, I can't begin to tell you how hard it was for the families. The deprivation was enormous and although the conditions at Gresford were extremely difficult people would be reluctant to pack that up as there were no other jobs on offer anywhere. Unemployment stood at 41% in the Wrexham area, socially the majority of working people were a very deprived class.

Now although they had this quota of coal, if for some reason they hadn't got their quota out they were able to bring people back on a Friday night to work extra - anything to satisfy the profit margins. This was one of the reasons that on that Friday night in 1934 there were more people in Gresford than normal. Another reason for the deprivation, was all the other people who were having their share out of the profits. Besides, the workers and the colliery owners, there were the landowners who had to be paid a royalty. The truth of it was that the person who owned the land owned the royalties on the coal. Successive governments since the 1920's had looked at the 'royalties situation' to see if there was any way round it, but as so many people would have been affected there was no easy solution, that is, until the end of the War. Another added expense, of having to pay royalties, which in turn affected the profits and so affected the workers, was having to pay a dead rent for coal they hadn't yet worked but wanted to take an option on. For example the Dennis section of the pit, which was mostly under Gresford village and beyond the church would also have been accessible to Llay Main colliery because they were working in an adjoining area. Gresford and Llay Main pits were working on either side of Gresford church.

This could have led to Lord Kenyon, who owned all this particular land, offering the rights to the Llay Main colliery if Gresford had not paid the dead rent, which they had been doing since 1918, approximately £3,000 a year. As Gresford colliery owners were paying this dead rent they would want the men to get into this area as quickly as possible. They needed to start producing coal from there to maximise their holdings to be making some sort of profit.

The deputies had " Authority without Responsibility". The colliery company themselves delegated the authority for running the different districts underground to the workmen in many instances, they subcontracted out, this resulted in an inability of the workmen themselves to share out fairly what could have a reasonable wage. The subcontracting system that applied here was the Charter system, which meant that a man was created the Chartermaster, he would draw the money on the Friday night and he was supposed to share it out. He would have the say in who was hired or fired, he might not work for three or four days but as it was his section, he had the money for it.

We finished here as Ithel's grandson arrived to visit but not before Ithel told me that I had to look at all of this DISPASSIONATELY.

"There were those who were dead against the management and those who were dead against the workmen. You have to tell the truth as you see it, from the facts, warts and all. If you are going to do it, do it right.
We have a responsibility, you and I, unless it is a novel you are writing, to tell the facts, so that people who come, after you and I have gone, can get the facts of what happened - not a one-sided lefty view."

Ithel Kelly died aged 67 and a large funeral service was held for him at Gresford Church.

CHAPTER 6
The Gresford Letters

The Past is a foreign country: they do things differently there.[53]

Reading the letters that were written in response to the mining disaster at Gresford Colliery on September 22nd, 1934, reminds us that this episode in history, once, was real life and grants us a valuable insight into not only what life was like then, but also an awareness of the values and compassionate spirit, held by so many people, in a time of great distress. It is interesting to note that of the 10,000 or so letters that were received in North Wales at this time, so many were from men and women living in the North of England, other coal-mining areas, and from the designated 'depressed areas' where the people were no strangers themselves, to adversity, hardship and sorrow.

These letters offer a glimpse of life in the 1930's, an unfettered response to a disaster that touched the lives of so many people, not only in Great Britain but expatriates, especially Welsh men and women living abroad. Many of the 'Gresford letters' appear to be written with an impulsive immediacy, prompted by the enormity of the disaster and its inherent consequences, for all the miners and their families in this part of the North-East Wales coalfield, creating a sense of "intimate contact" as if they were speaking to us directly.

The bulk of the personal letters were from women, with little regard to formality or with literary expertise, especially when they were writing with regard to adoption or the care of the "fatherless children", - imparting more to us than any official document or social history. The conversational use of language in the the letters, positions us to identify with the experiences and feelings delineated in this correspondence. And yet we, as readers, are also voyeuristic in our 'seeking out' of every little detail of emotion, 'truth' and 'fact' contained in these letters.

However, I feel that I have to immediately contradict myself here because, as a writer and storyteller, I recognise the fact that the official and semi-official letters "tell the story" in a different way. We understand the enormous task of the Joint Secretaries of the Relief Fund, whilst we read, time after time, that the letters will be put before 'the Committee', or 'at the next meeting', of another particular Committee.

71

There were only so many ways of saying thank you, and deflecting questions that no one had the answers to, then, or six months after. The rich were still rich, demanding and expecting the respect that their position or standing afforded them; and the poor were still poor, hoping for, rather than expecting, anything.

I have concentrated on the correspondence and documentation held at the Flintshire Records Office at Hawarden in the records of the Gresford Colliery Disaster Relief Fund. As the collection represents not only "the details of the setting up and administration of the relief fund but the records of an enormous response, locally, nationally and internationally to a 'major industrial disaster,'"[54] the documentation shows its importance in the context of the British Coal-Mining Industry and economy in this particular area of North East Wales during the 1930's.

As so many of the personal letters were written, by women, had these documents been destroyed along with the other records appertaining to Gresford Colliery, during the nationalisation of the coal industry in 1947, an important part of women's history would have been lost forever instead of being "hidden from history"[55] as it has been up to now, quite literally buried and forgotten in the Flintshire archives.
Man is an historical animal, with a deep sense of his own past: and if he cannot integrate the past by a history explicit and true, he will integrate it by a history implicit and false. The challenge is one which no historian with any conviction of the value of his work can ignore: and the way to meet it is not to evade the issue of 'relevance', but to accept the fact and work out its implications.[56]

These letters, which play a central role in the coal-mining history of Wrexham in the 1930's, are only part of the jigsaw of this momentous event, without them there would be more gaps and silences leaving us with an "implicit and false history" of the Gresford Colliery disaster. There are so many unanswered questions, that it is fortuitous, for us, to have these letters enabling us to observe for ourselves the ways in which people showed their unanimity with those of Gresford Colliery.

Arthur Marwick, in *Nature of History*[57], contends that surviving documentary evidence *such as letters* [my italics] are especially valuable because; they are not deliberately designed for the benefit of the historian and so can be seen as the objective residue of the past, they provide the historian with the unwitting testimony of people in the past.

Nevertheless these letters do not speak for themselves, my task then, is to objectively,'revive in imagination the whole of that series of acts performed by the author of the document'[58],and by choosing a selection of letters and categorising them in a particular way, these letters can be placed in context and an understanding of their meaning and significance be achieved.

The letters were firstly segregated into personal/individual, public/private, official/semi-official, offers/requests. I had intended to further segregate them according to gender, age, position, nationality and class, but for clarity and simplicity I opted for classifications which were self-explanatory, with limited critique or guidance from me where necessary, leaving the reader to come to her own conclusions. My classifications in the main body of the text are as follows:

i. State: Letters from the King and Queen and the Prince of Wales to the Lord Lieutenants of Denbighshire and Flintshire, and their replies. (These are the only letters to and from Royalty lodged at the Records Office, signifying an immediate high profile/involvement but also signifying their lack of involvement after that.)

ii. Official: Here I have included letters from various Councils writing in their capacity as representatives of their townspeople. All the letters, without exception, were written by men.

iii. Semi-Official: The letters included in this section are representative of voluntary organisations, the Church and various institutions and denote a cross section of society, male and female from working and middle class backgrounds.

iv. Personal: Under this heading I have added various sub-headings, to enable the reader to identify the numerous people who wrote with their contributions, requests and suggestions. Again there are letters from a cross section of society, mostly working class women offering their contributions of clothing or small monetary donations.

v. Women and Children: The letters contained in this section cover many aspects concerning the widows and their families. Predominantly the concerns were for the adoption of any orphans and the well-being of the women and their families, however several individuals appear to have had selfish motives of their own, where the benefit to the dependant of the disaster was a secondary consideration.

The Letters

STATE - Royal

A telegram was received by the Lord Lieutenant of Denbighshire, from the King at Balmoral, 22nd September, 1934:

The Queen and I are grieved to hear of the disaster at Gresford Colliery this morning. We feel deeply for the miners involved and the terrible sorrow and anxiety of their families and friends. Please convey to all this message of our heartfelt sympathy, and keep me informed as to the gallant efforts being made to reach the miners.

G R I.

The Lord Lieutenant also received the following message from the Prince of Wales:

I am deeply distressed to hear of the terrible disaster at Gresford Colliery. Please convey my sincerest sympathy to the relatives of those who have lost their lives in this tragic manner. Edward. P.

The Lord Lieutenant's reply to the King.

On behalf of the miners involved in the disaster at Gresford Colliery and their families and friends, I have the honour to thank your Majesties for the gracious and most sympathetic message just received. The rescuers are gallantly continuing their determined efforts to reach the 102 men known to be entrapped in the mine. I regret to inform your Majesties that two of the rescuers have lost their lives in rescue work and the ascertained number of deaths is 9.

Within two days the Lord Lieutenant had to inform their Majesties that the disaster had in fact taken a far worse toll than was at first thought:

Telegram sent to the King by Mr R C Roberts, (solicitor and Clerk to the Lieutenancy) on behalf of the Lord Lieutenant of Denbighshire.

It is with regret that I have to inform your Majesties that the management of the Gresford Colliery, the Miner's representatives and your Majesties' Inspectors have decided that owing to conditions now existing in the mine it is not possible that any of the men entrapped in the mine can be alive. Owing to continuous explosions today and the danger arising there from it was also decided to withdraw all working parties from the mine. The death roll is expected to considerably exceed the original estimate.

Mr Roberts was also responsible for a letter sent on the 24th September 1934 to the Lord Mayor of London's secretary on behalf of Lord Gladstone of Hawarden, the Lord Lieutenant of Flintshire:

..the Lord Mayor desires a statement as to the position in connection with the sad disaster at Gresford Colliery should be forwarded to him by tonight's post. We are accordingly enclosing herewith a rough statement setting forth certain facts which may be helpful to the Lord Mayor in broadcasting his appeal for donations to the Relief Fund. We consider that the information contained in three evening papers which circulate in the district of the accident might be also helpful to the Lord Mayor.....

Unfortunately Mr Roberts did not have official numbers to hand and in effect could be blamed for the subsequent reports, appeals and influx of letters concerning the 800 fatherless children, when in fact there were '166' widows, '241' children and '209' dependants left behind.[59]

Part of the "rough statement" which Mr Roberts refers to follows:

... As far as can be ascertained at present there are two hundred widows and eight hundred fatherless children in addition to aged parents and dependents. As a result of this disaster the pit itself will be closed down for several months, so that the whole of the working population at the pit and the larger population of dependents have a very dark outlook for the coming winter, no other evenue (sic) of employment being open to them. When the pit re-opens there will be many months work on which a comparatively small number of men only can be employed. A period of unemployment must face many men when the reconditioning of the pit begins several months hence. A population of seven to eight thousand people will constitute a distressed area for the next year. The need of many of the children of the men killed will not only be immediate, but there will be a period in the future when many of these fatherless children will attain the age of fourteen and fifteen when provision should be made to enable them to make a start in life because long before that time any legal compensation to which they may become entitled will have been exhausted.

This memorandum was sent only two days after the disaster took place and the inaccuracies it contains can only have been assumptions on the part of Mr Roberts or the Lord Lieutenant (on whose behalf Mr Roberts was writing), as it was far too early for them to know exactly what had happened, or was going to happen. This, effectively false, information was broadcast to the nation and run by many newspapers which resulted in the overwhelming response evident in the letters that follow in this chapter:

The night of the wireless appeal a hat was taken round, and I understand between £5 and £6 was collected - a very fine, spontaneous act I thought. (Personal letter from a vicar to a Councillor Rogers of Wrexham 30.9.34)

The ideological representation of this information in the "serious" newspapers, as well as in the tabloids and on the radio, lent this "myth" a believable aura of truth, for instance, If Royalty was responding to this news by contributing a large donation then the details portrayed must be "true." This ideologically constructed myth, by omitting facts and selecting the truth, could be seen as a political act if one considers the economics of the 1930's, in the aftermath of "the Depression", when the "knowledge" of another persons misfortune helped detract from their own dire circumstances. The response to these "myths" perpetrated by newspaper reporting, is evident in the letters such as the one from the Town Clerk from Bishop's Castle who alluded to statements concerning the widows of the Gresford miners receiving £600 in compensation in addition to their widow's pension (see letters under Official heading), and another from The St. David's Welsh Society of Ottawa writing a week after the disaster and

were deeply shocked on reading the sad news..........hoping against hope that the number of lives lost would not be so heavy as at first reported. (see letters From Overseas.)

OFFICIAL - Councils

Well over eleven hundred Councils wrote in reply to a circular from the Mayor of Wrexham and the Joint Secretaries of the Fund, many sent their condolences, desiring to express their deepest sympathy with the relatives and dependants of those who lost their lives in the disaster, others sent contributions, "herewith a cheque value 100 guineas and I hope to send you a further sum within the course of a few days" (Mayor of Wisbech 9.10.34).

The Mayor of Warrington sent a cheque for £300, being a *"first instalment ... and extend our heartfelt sympathies with those neighbours of yours who have lost their menfolk under such tragic circumstances;*

76

and we sincerely trust that our gesture will assist in lightening the burden of sorrow and hardship which I know will be the lot of many in and around Gresford".

Other Councils sent details of the funds they were initiating and asked in what way others were subscribing. The Mayor of Jarrow, Durham sent this letter on the 28th September 1934, expressing sympathy and sending a donation, even though his own townspeople were in need themselves:
Dear Mr Mayor
I am desired by the Council of this Borough to convey through you, their horror at the appalling disaster which occasioned the death of 264 workmen at Gresford Colliery, and to extend the heartfelt sympathy of this Borough with the relatives and dependents of the deceased men. The people of the Borough suffered, during the comparatively short period in which Jarrow Pit was working, several colliery disasters including two in which 82 lives were lost, and they have lived unfortunately near to other even more serious disasters. My townspeople, are, therefore vividly aware of the distress which must exist in the town of Wrexham and surrounding districts, and the dire need in which some of the inhabitants must be, and although, owing to the extraordinary distress through prolonged unemployment which this town is suffering, the desire is felt to give what small assistance is possible towards those who are at the present in the greater need. Accordingly, I am enclosing a cheque for £10 towards the relief fund which you are organising, and I trust that your efforts may be successful so that the relatives and dependents may at least be saved the extremity of poverty

The Clerk to Ebbw Vale Urban District Council, writing on behalf of the people of a coal mining area, who had also had their fair share of hardship and unemployment;

I am enclosing a cheque for £114:1:10 as a Town's contribution to the Fund. The sum, I know, is not a large one but having regard to the severe depression from which this district has suffered for many years I think it may be regarded as a true indication of the people's appreciation and sympathy with the relatives of those who lost their lives at the Gresford Colliery.

Other Councils wanted to know more details and raised questions that were being asked nationally;
8th October, 1934.

Dear Sir

Adverting to your circular letter of the 29th ultimo, appealing to the Council to organise collections, etc., in their area, and requesting co-operation in making the Relief Fund as large as possible, I would state that the question will be considered by my Council at their next meeting on Tuesday evening next. In the meantime, I would like to be furnished with as much information as possible as to how the dependants of the deceased miners will eventually be compensated. Will they be compensated under the Workmen's Compensation Acts, or in any other way? if not, will their future be entirely dependent on the Relief Fund? Also, I shall be glad, if possible, to be informed generally how it will be proposed to disburse the Relief Fund.

Town Clerk, Borough of Acton.

The reply, two days later:

...... the dependents will certainly receive compensation under the Workmen's Compensation Act, which, as you know, will   practically exhaust itself when the dependents reach the age of 15 years. The Fund is now being used to meet cases of distress, which are   investigated by a Committee, and who have personal interviews with those affected, but in a month's time it is hoped that sufficient information will be available to place the Fund on an actuarial basis.

Actuaries were appointed to calculate the insurance risks and premiums so that the beneficiaries would hold policies to provide funds for their lifetime and also to cover their funeral expenses.[60]

The Clerk to Urmston Urban District Council, Manchester also had a similar enquiry when informing the Secretaries of his Council's fundraising efforts, as to the possibility of "utilising funds which had been raised in the past." The Secretaries replied that it was proposed to place the Gresford Relief Fund on an actuarial basis.

The Town Clerk from Bishop's Castle in Shropshire, on the 6th October, informed the Joint Secretaries that his Mayor had started a Fund and that he would be sending 'a remittance' at the end of the month. In his postscript he had a request:

The Mayor is constantly met with statements that each of the widows of the men killed in the Disaster will get £600 and a Widows' pension; also that there are thousands of pounds in Wrexham which were surplus to the requirements of the last disaster. Of course we know that £600 is only the maximum Workmen's Compensation in exceptional circumstances, but the Mayor would be glad of a letter from you replying to these objections, so that he can have definite evidence.

to which the secretaries replied;

With regard to the postscript, we would point out that, of course, compensation will be paid to the widows under the Workmen's Compensation Act, but, as you will know, compensation money is invested in the Post Office Savings Bank, and monthly allowances are allocated to the widow towards the maintenance of herself and family. This Fund will exhaust itself when each dependent child arrives at the age of 15 years of age, and would not itself be enough to maintain the widows and dependents under ordinary circumstances. Again, from 15 years to 18 years the youths could hardly be expected to maintain themselves on what they would be able to earn, as at this stage of life, the children will miss the breadwinner as much as at any other time. There is certainly no amount surplus to requirement.

Not all Councils were so forthcoming, a few Councils could or would not assist;

Your letter of the 29th ultimo was considered by my Council at its meeting held last evening when I was directed to state that in view of the pressing need of the Distressed Areas Scheme it is regretted that no assistance can be given to your fund.

Clerk to the Council, Sevenoaks.

Tilbury Urban District Council went one step further in their refusal to contribute ;

..... it is my Council's opinion, however, that the welfare of the widows and children of miners who lose their lives in the course of their employment, whether in great disasters or in the daily loss of life in the mines, should not be a matter upon which it is necessary to make public appeal. My Council are strongly of the opinion that such relief as is necessary should be a charge in the first instant upon the Mining Industry and if and so far as the Industry is unable to make adequate provision, then to the National Funds.

Although these letters, fell into the category of open-archive, official / state, at the time they were written, may have been closed or restricted access, which leads one to suspect that the opinions stated were often those of a few individuals rather than the majority they represented, few people would be privy to the correspondence written by the Councils. Letters, like the one from Tilbury, stuck in my mind and when I came to read other types of letters, personal and from works and institutions, I found that individuals were sometimes saying something quite different. Occasionally the author would appear politically motivated, others wanting to get a message across, others, in sympathy, just had to write.

SEMI-OFFICIAL
I have used this term in the broadest sense to include Churches, Institutions, Organisations for instance, where the letter is representative of a number of individuals. The reader tends to make assumptions as to the class of people and the gender represented.

Churches, Institutions and Organisations.
There were countless letters from Women's Institutes, Associations, Branches of Labour Parties, Guilds, Church Guilds, Girl Guides, and Women's sections of numerous firms and companies, who wished to be acknowledged in their own right as remembering their "Sisters in North Wales." They sent their deepest sympathy, donations of money, clothing etc wanting "to be in touch with the women who have suffered owing to the disaster."
The Women's Section of Bentley Labour Party, themselves in a coalmining area, were one of the first to write, 24.9.34;

To our Sisters of North Wales
Please accept the loving sympathy of the Women of Bentley in your great sorrow. Words are cold comfort but our hearts go out to you, having passed thro' the same experience.(45 lives lost on 20.11.31) May God in His mercy strengthen, sustain and comfort each one of you is our earnest prayer.

The Women's Guild of the Congregational Union of England and Wales sent their condolences with a donation and the Women's section of Hemsden Methodist Chapel whose husbands were employed at the Chislet Colliery, Canterbury, prayed *"that the thought that one day we shall all meet our dear ones again would bring a little comfort to those sorrowing."*

The North Wales Women's Temperance Union who were federated to the National British Women's Total Abstinence Union, sent a donation of £10 and The County Secretary of the Denbigh County Federation of Women's Institutes representing 36 WI's, wrote at great length offering their practical expression of sympathy. The Girl Guides of the County of Denbighshire also wished to offer practical sympathy by *"adopting a family"* to whom they could promise *"a regular supply of groceries and other commodities, instead of sending a cash contribution to the fund."*

The Tow Law Women's Institute forwarded their donation from:
"one of the distressed mining areas, standing high above sea level in the County of Durham....We do hope your funds will increase more and more and that the relatives will be able to obtain a certain amount of comfort to compensate them a little for the great loss they have sustained. I wish the amount we are sending was much larger but 90% of the population are out of work."

The Welsh National Women's Auxiliary, (whose object was to supplement the work of the Welsh Council of Young Men's Christian Associations)
.....offered their most heartfelt sympathy and;
we would like you to know how deeply we feel, each one of us personally, and how as a Welsh Association our hearts extend in sympathy and understanding to our fellow men and women in North Wales.

The Rotary Club of Doncaster sent a cheque and
...deepest sympathies...... perhaps situated as we are in a mining area, which too has had its catastrophes, we can realise better than many how great is the incidence (sic) of the blow, which has fallen with such suddenness on your people. So the measure of our knowledge is also that of our great regret.

Many Welsh people living away from the Principality were especially affected by the knowledge of the disaster, particularly those who had moved from a coalmining area to live in England or overseas. A solicitor in London wrote the following letter on 2nd October 1934 to the Mayor of Wrexham explaining that he had approached every Welsh Society in London concerning the Gresford appeal:
I have to report that I have sent an Appeal to every member of the Denbighshire Society in London and to every member of the Gwynedd Lodge...............It is too early for us to receive the donations of the various Societies as the officials have not yet had time to meet between last Thursday and today. I am glad to say, however, that the Treasurer has already received in cash up to date the sum of £136.

WELSH NATIONAL WOMEN'S AUXILIARY

PRESIDENT: THE COUNTESS OF PLYMOUTH.

VICE-PRESIDENTS:

OBJECT : TO SUPPLEMENT THE WORK OF THE WELSH NATIONAL COUNCIL OF YOUNG MEN'S CHRISTIAN ASSOCIATIONS

HEADQUARTERS: 53, PARK PLACE, CARDIFF.

CORNBOROUGH,

PORTHCAWL

Oct 5.

Dear Sir,

At a general meeting of the above Society held yesterday - it was the unanimous wish that I should send you our most heartfelt sympathy in the recent tradjedy which occured at Gresham Colliery -

We would like you to know how deeply we feel, each one of us personally, & how as a Welch Association our hearts extend in sympathy & understanding to our fellow men & women in North Wales -

Yours v. sincerely
Margaret Cope!

Letter from The Welsh National Women's Auxiliary

THE COMMUNIST PARTY OF Gt. BRITAIN

(British Section of the Communist International)

READ:
DAILY WORKER
One Penny

COMMUNIST REVIEW
Monthly   Sixpence

16 KING STREET, COVENT GARDEN,
LONDON - - - W.C.2.

Telephone: Temple Bar 4277

CENTRAL EXECUTIVE COMMITTEE

All communications to be addressed to the Secretariat and not to individuals

22.9.34

The Secretary,
North Wales Miners Ascooiation,
Wrexham.

Dear Comrade,

I am instructed by the Central Committee of the Communist Party to convey to your members and their families , our deepest sympathy in the terrible disaster that has taken place at the Gresford Colliery.

We solmenly pledge ourselves to work harder than ever before to build up the unity of the miners in order that they can obtain better conditions in regard to safety precautions, working conditions, higher wages and shorter hours.

Especially will we work to try and strenghten the fight of the Welsh miners who are at this very moment demanding improvement in their conditions. The loss of hundreds of miners in Gresford, the misery and untold anguish in hundreds of homes, brings out once again the danger and insecurity of the miners calling, and starvation wages they receive.

The whole working class must now be organised to help the miners to bring an end to this intolerable state of affairs, and also to immediately launch a nation wide campaign to come to the relief of those who have lost their breadwinners, and those who are injured.

This is the olny way in which reparation can be made to the victims of Mining Capitalism.

Yours fraternally,

[signature]

For the Centeral Committee of
The Communist Party of Great Britian.

[signature]

For the Centeral Committee of

This letter from The Communist Party of Great Britain was one of the first received by the Miner's Association, as it was written the day of the disaster, 22nd September, 1934;

Dear Comrade,
I am instructed by the Central Committee of the Communist Party to convey to your members and their families, our deepest sympathy in the terrible disaster that has taken place at the Gresford Colliery. We solemnly pledge ourselves to work harder than ever before to build up the unity of the miners in order that they can obtain better conditions in regard to safety precautions, working conditions, higher wages and shorter hours. Especially will we work to try and strengthen the fight of the Welsh miners who are at this very moment demanding improvement in their conditions. The loss of hundreds of miners at Gresford, the misery and untold anguish in hundreds of homes, brings out once again the danger and insecurity of the miners calling, and starvation wages they receive. The whole working class must now be organised to help the miners to bring an end to this intolerable state of affairs, and also to immediately launch a nation wide campaign to come to the relief of those who have lost their breadwinners, and those who are injured. This is the olny (sic) way in which reparation can be made to the victims of Mining Capitalism. Yours fraternally,

The COLNE BRANCH of the Labour League of Youth and the Newcastle-Staffs & Trades & Labour Council also wrote in a similar vein: (see opposite page)
The following resolution was passed, in silence by all the delegates, at the Annual Conference of The League of Industry at the end of September 1934, and a donation of £62.14.7d was given "to relieve immediate necessities":

The Conference of the League of Industry expresses .. *its deepest sympathy with the bereaved families of the miners who lost their lives in the terrible pit disaster at the Gresford Colliery. As fellow industrialists we appreciate the dangers of the miners' calling an in the interests of the living miners and future generations we express the strong hope that the resources of science will be exploited to the full to prevent the recurrence of such devastating calamities.*

PERSONAL

It is the fervent prayer of everyone who has worked in the mines that something will be done to bring home to the minds of each person in our country - The Price of Coal. A London Bus Driver. (ex-miner.) 29.9.34

Dear Sir,

The COLNE BRANCH OF THE LABOUR LEAGUE OF YOUTH at their meeting held last tuesday evening Sept 25th instructed me to write you expressing their great sorrow at the terrible catastrophe which has fallen upon your town, it is indeed tragic to think of the many children rendered fatherless , of the many poor women who are now widows and in some cases losing sons as well, all in the space of a few hours. We in the LABOUR MOVEMENT maintain that the conditions under which a miner lives should be thoroughly overhaul overhauled and all risks eliminated as far as possible regardless of expence , human lives are worth far far more than any amount of mony and to think that 274 lives ,lives which belong to the Great working class, should be blotted out in this manner, these and their comrades in other trades have to take many risks in the pursuit of their employment despite the fact that scienceand our knowledge in general is supposed to have increased, many people seem to hold human lives far to cheap today and it is always the people of the working class who

have to suffer, we would welcome the day when all people can live in perfect safety and comfort . You will find enclosed P.O. for Five-Shillings we know it is not a large sum, our movement (LEAGUE OF YOUTH) has not been in existence in Colne very long therefore our funds are not very large but we are sure that any sum no matter how small will be welcome as it will be urgerently needed, once again expressing our sorrow

On behalf of the Members of the LEAGUE OF YOUTH

I Remain your's Fraternally

W. BAILEY(SEC)

20, Church Meadows

Colne

5/-

The Rev. Tom Jones,
Berse Vicarage,
Near Wrexham.

£52 - 10/-

My dear Tom,

It was unfortunate that I was not able to have a chat with you when I passed through Wrexham on Tuesday. I was going to talk to you about the Gresford Colliery Disaster.

I feel this terrible catastrophe in quite a personal way. As a child I was brought up and spent 25 years of my early life in Wales, and I know something of the miners and their families. I therefore feel in duty bound to send a donation towards the relief of these 800 women and children who have been left unprovided for.

I thought, at one time, of sending my small cheque to the "Montgomeryshire Express" towards their Fund, or to the Lord Mayor of London's Fund, but I feel I would like you personally to hand over my cheque for 50 guineas enclosed herewith to the Mayor of Wrexham for his Fund, and I do hope that the Public generally will respond generously.

With my love to Winnie and the youngsters,

yours affectionately,

Shown on the previous page, Edwin King wrote to the vicar of Berse, although there were nothing like 800 women and children to be cared for his heart was in the right place.

On the 14th October 1913, at the Universal Colliery in Senghenydd, Glamorgan the worst disaster in British Coalmining history took place with a loss of 439 lives, so the receipt of the following letter is extremely poignant.(1.10.34.)

Dear Sir

Please accept enclosed P.O. 15/- towards your relief fund for the dependants of Gresford Colliery Explosion. We are a family who have not

Senghenydd.
Oct. 1st 1934.   Caerphilly.
                                        Glam.   15/-

Hon. Treasurer.
    Gresford Colliery relief fund.
    Dear Sir.
        Please accept enclosed P.O. 15/-
towards your relief fund for the
dependants of Gresford Colliery
Explosion.
            We are a family who have
not forgotten the horrors of Oct. 14th
1913. when we lost our dear son
& brother, at a very tender age. (14)
            Our deepest sympathy goes
out to the bereaved families, we
know, alas! too well, the suffering
they endure.
                Yours with deepest
    sympathy

forgotten the horrors of Oct 14th 1913 when we lost our dear son and brother, at a very tender age of 14. Our deepest sympathy goes out to the bereaved families, we know, Alas! too well, the suffering they endure.

Yours with deepest sympathy, W.E and Family.

Suggestions as to how the Fund should be distributed.

Progress, far from consisting in change, depends on retentiveness...
Those who do not remember the past are condemned to repeat it.[61]

Many people wrote to the respective Mayors of Wrexham and London and the Joint Secretaries with their suggestions of how the money received for the Fund should be best distributed and commented about how others had used/not used their funds. A gentleman 'echoed' the sentiment expressed concerning the sufferers;

Mill Park Avenue

Hornchurch

Essex

25. 9. 34

The Hon. Treasurer

Gresford (Wrexham) Colliery Disaster Fund

Dear Sir

Kindly accept the enclosed small contribution of 5/= to your fund and I sincerely hope that many such contributions from people who have not much to give will be received by you.

It is always a matter of surprise to me why those who are engaged in the most necessary occupation for human welfare – as it is certainly the most hazardous – should be left to fight their grim battle in comparative poverty.

Yours faithfully

...it is always a matter of surprise to me why those who are engaged in the most necessary occupation for human welfare - as it is certainly the most hazardous - should be left to fight their grim battle in comparative poverty.

And the organiser of a collection at Rossendale, Lancashire wanted assurance before he forwarded the money that;

the money is being distributed at once. You will appreciate that it is unfair to ask working-people to contribute to funds that are administered as many charities in the past have been. That is funds held up for months when people need it most and often the bulk of the money never distributed at all. We feel that when the bread-winner has been taken, or employment been lost in a tragedy of this sort money cannot be given to them indiscriminately.

The reply from the Joint Secretaries was short and to the point: *'we are directed to inform you that the monies received are being distributed according to the need.'*

A newspaper cutting alleging "IDLE MONEY - Huge Surplus from Relief Funds" was sent by a well wisher from Southport to the Mayor of Wrexham in the hope that by bringing this 'fact' to the Mayor's attention he would be able to draw upon this money for the Gresford Fund. The newspaper report highlighted the comments of the President of the Lancashire and Cheshire Miners Federation, Mr J McGuirk who said that he had asked the Government:

..to create a central authority to take charge of all surplus funds from these old relief subscriptions and to apply them for the immediate relief of sufferers when disasters like that at Wrexham occur. The Government has the power to do it, but it refuses to take action. Moreover, it will not give us any reason for its refusal.[62]

Another well-wisher, sent a cutting from The Observer 6.10.34 of a letter from the Mayor of Chester to the Editor with his suggestion as to what should be done with 'surplus relief funds', with a hope that the Relief Fund Committee would not copy the mistakes of other Fund holders.

Nine days after the disaster at Gresford, a director of a Patent Ship-Log Manufacturers in Birmingham informed the Town Clerk of Wrexham that his employees were making a subscription to the Gresford Fund and he enquired:

May we ask what you anticipate will be required to take care of all the dependents, and the amount of money that has now come to hand?

88

The Town Clerk took great pains to answer this letter outlining as best he could how a neighbouring colliery had dealt with their disaster funds.

Contributions and Offers of Clothing and Kind.
People responded in whatever way they could, sending their: "last sixpence" ('A Winsford Unemployed Family'), 'a Working man from Hull' enclosed P O 2/6, *"with feeling too deep to discribe (sic) of this awful calamity to my fellow men and their dependants ... A little help is worth a world of sympathy,"* and a pensioner admitted to going without her dinner for three days to send a few pennies. Many of the donations were anonymous - " three sympathisers," "an old age pensioner," "an old Miner," " two grandchildren of a Staffordshire miner," " Yours with a full heart," " from a little Welsh girl in London," " from a sympathetic family," "an old Wrexhamite," and " in memory of a father who was a deputy."

Other letters were signed or written with more familiarity, *"From Gwennie Willis of Portsmouth aged 7 yrs who is very, very sorry for all the poor little girls and boys who have no daddies."* (6d was enclosed), from *"just a few working pals. May God Comfort and relieve every Mother, widow and child in their great sorrow is the prayer of; Nell, Millie, Ruth, Dots, Roy, Mother and Myself. We will remember them. God Bless you all, Dorothy Gregory."* R J Jones of Newtown (below) explained that he had *"been laid up through illness for three years"* but still hoped to be able to

25/9/34

Dear Sir
    Please accept my small contribution. I have been laid up throu illness three years, but I have still hopes to be able to come to support my family, but there are poor souls around you that have no hopes of their breadwinner to return
    My greatest sorrow is that my contribution is so small but its sent with best of feelings to those that are more in need....

come to support his family, *" but there are poor souls around you that have no hope of their breadwinner to return,"* he sent a postal order for 2/-, *"with the best of feelings to those that are more in need."*

A few who wished to send their donations direct asked for names and addresses of dependants, offering such as *"two warm coats and a warm jumper for someone during the cold weather, also some papers for the children to look at and read, it will divert their minds from their trouble."* A local bakery in Wrexham sent fifty pounds with *"no objection to our contribution being used to alleviate distress in some other local colliery accident, where the sufferers are not eligible for relief under the present scheme."*

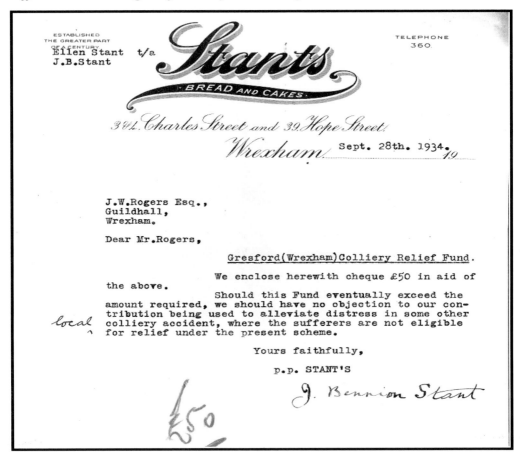

ESTABLISHED THE GREATER PART OF A CENTURY.

Ellen Stant t/a
J.B.Stant

Stants
· BREAD AND CAKES ·

TELEPHONE 360.

3 & 4. Charles Street and 39. Hope Street.

Wrexham. Sept. 28th. 1934. 19

J.W.Rogers Esq.,
Guildhall,
Wrexham.

Dear Mr.Rogers,

Gresford(Wrexham)Colliery Relief Fund.

We enclose herewith cheque £50 in aid of the above.

Should this Fund eventually exceed the amount required, we should have no objection to our con-tribution being used to alleviate distress in some other *local* colliery accident, where the sufferers are not eligible for relief under the present scheme.

Yours faithfully,

p.p. STANT'S

J. Bennion Stant

£50

What is not clear from this letter is whether they were referring to sufferers of a colliery accident that had happened or in respect of one that should happen in the future. Perhaps working in the Coal Industry came with expected life threatening possibilities, that people living and working in the vicinity of a colliery came to accept?.

The workers who have perished were always admired as a portion of the working class fighting against damnable odds.

The Devons Parade, L.M.S. Steam
Sheds, Bow, E.3.

Many of the donations and contributions were listed in the Press, in most cases it was just the name and amount, or details of the contribution. Newspapers set up their own Funds to enable their readers to contribute, within days of the disaster the Daily Mirror had sent £20,000. The Express and Star wrote of their successful appeal on the 15th October, 1934, *"We have pleasure in enclosing a cheque for £3,125.3.2, being the final cheque for our Fund in connection with the Gresford Colliery Disaster; making a total of £8,125.3.2."* Daily Herald readers were urged to help by sending donations of money and clothing, and the Exmouth Chronicle gave their appeal front-page status. The Editor of The Evening Post and The Jersey Weekly Post was so proud of his readers who had subscribed a total of £1077.2.6 that he wrote to the Mayor asking if he would personally write to the readers via the columns of the papers; *"the magnificent sum of £1077.2.6 subscribed by a small community of 50,000 inhabitants so far removed from the scene of the disaster is deserving of some special recognition."* (see too letters from Overseas.)

Those who could not send money offered assistance, clothing and foodstuffs opening their hearts and their homes to help in some way. The Aber Valley Choral Society of Senghenydd had *"unfortunately experienced two similar disasters in their village, the memory of which still clings but wanted to hold a concert in aid of the Gresford Appeal"*, and a Mrs Heys wrote from Stockport in October to say that she and others were promoting a concert on behalf of the Gresford Colliery Relief Fund, for which they required authority to claim exemption from Entertainments Duty, and would the Secretaries *"kindly forward the necessary authority to the Collector of Custom and Excise at Sheffield."* This was one of many "concerts" organised in aid of the Fund.

Mr G W Thompson on behalf of Pant and District Angling Association had written to request help with his concert, and on the 6th October the Manager of the Ann Boleyn Hotel in Hythe, Staines wrote this letter with a similar request to the Managing Director of Gresford Colliery, Mr Henry Dyke Dennis ;

Dear Sir

It is useless to try and tell you how deeply touched the whole peoples of the South have been through the recent terrible disaster and being a Northerner myself I am anxious to do all in my power towards assisting in the relief of distress. I am organising a big Carnival Ball on October 19th at the Staines Town Hall and a street and theatre collection on

Saturday October 20th. I wondered if it were possible for one of the rescuers to come down here to assist in that way......

Henry Dyke Dennis contacted the Miner's Representatives who sent two miners to assist, which proved very successful and a cheque for £91.7.4 was forwarded to the Lord Mayor's Fund. Various concerts and evenings of entertainment were organised at workingmen's clubs up and down the country.

Donations of clothing started arriving from all over the country, a lady from West Wickham in Kent wanted to know the name and address of a distressed family where there was a girl *"about five foot tall."* She did not want to send the clothes to *"a Depot"* preferring *"to get in touch personally with the family."* The Secretaries wrote to say it would be best if the clothes were sent to the Lady Mayoress for her Ladies Committee to distribute the clothes to the *" best possible advantage."* Many women sent clothing with a little note attached, *"I am a widow having to earn my living so cannot afford to send money, but thought these articles might come in for some woman if only as working garments."* Another widow wrote:

A Wallasey widow has sent by parcel post a parcel containing a dress (with extra material), a jacket - two hats- which she hopes may be acceptable to some needy mourner. Whilst another Widow, a Mother of nine, sent clothes, because she was *"unable to give money."* A gentleman sent a parcel enclosing *"a suit which may be of some use to somebody in your bereaved town."*

It would have been a tremendous additional task for the Secretaries to reply to every letter they received, the only noticeable pattern I have found in their replies to personal letters, is that of (the women) in the following cases, who used headed notepaper and /or wrote well. Some had a response within days of the disaster, others, some time after, so maybe the time element and the magnitude of their task, prevented the Secretaries from answering more, and I am being uncharitable in my thoughts.

A single lady wrote from Hampshire *" rejoicing to see how well the public are showing their feelings in this time of distress,"* she hoped that the funds would continue to "roll in." The Secretaries replied acknowledging her kindly interest towards the widows, orphans and dependants, and that, the clothing she had sent would be distributed by the Ladies Committee to *"the best possible advantage."* Two ladies sent clothing, one from Stoke on Trent, the other from London, with letters written on mourning stationery, black-edged notepaper, wanting to bring comfort to the sufferers, as they had lived in colliery districts in the past and were *"acutely aware of the miner's lot,"*... and could *" fully realise the horror and grimness of it all."*

Mrs Bennett and family from Cromer in Norfolk sent some boots that they had had mended, *"and quite a dear young boot mender charged me nothing for the mending, which touched us for the thoughtful kindness, he wished that to be his share, we wish we could do more."* J.E.J. sent garments and wrote simply, on monogrammed paper - *" I too have had a great and sudden bereavement. Mines and motors are terrible things."*

Contributions and Donations from Works.
From a Company in Old Ford, London, *"a parcel of 60/70 garments consisting of jacket and trousers, mostly serge, and we trust these will be useful,"* whilst another clothing Company sent, *" a bale containing dresses and underclothes for the little sufferers."* The women of a Laundry in London had made a collection from its one hundred or so employees and the manageress was especially pleased that having worked at the laundry for a number of years, *"everything that I have asked for from my superiors has been granted."* Also a Department Store in Camberwell, London who obviously supplied products by mail order, wrote to the Mayor of Wrexham asking for the names and addresses of the dependants as: *We have a large number of customers in the Wrexham area, and it is quite certain that some of these customers are in stricken circumstances following the catastrophe, and we would like to help by writing off our books any accounts which may be owing by such persons.*
This store was also able to advise the Mayor that they had already written off the debt of one woman, *"who writes us that her husband was one of the unfortunate men entombed."*

A telegram was received by the Mayor around November 1934, from the Northampton Boot Manufacturers who were prepared to replace boots of rescue parties, by March, the Town Clerk wrote that he had been unable to get a list of names and addresses (and boot sizes) and therefore felt that they would not be able to take advantage of the offer. Three hundred and thirty three boxes of, kippers and bloaters, were sent by a company in Aberdeen; *I caused a Fund to be started here in Aberdeen to help these poor people and felt that sending them a few hundred boxes of kippered herrings was doing them a good turn, It was a terrible calamity and we wish you every success in your endeavours to help them."*

ESTANDARTE BRAND.
ALCALDE BRAND.

DIRECTOR BRAND.
GERENTE BRAND.

TELEGRAMS—
"AMSMITH,"— ABERDEEN.

A. & M. SMITH LTD.

DIRECTORS.

SIR MALCOLM SMITH, K.B.E.
H. A. HOLMES.
J. I. WIGHT.
L. A. SMITH.
T. D. SMITH.

POST BOX 73.

ABERDEEN (SCOTLAND).

31st October, 1934.

The Joint Hon. Secretaries,
    Gresford(Wrexham)Colliery Disaster Relief Fund,
        County Buildings,
           WREXHAM.

Gentlemen,   KIPPERED HERRINGS.

    Yours 29th.

      Tomorrow we will despatch you 116 boxes Kippers and
17 boxes Bloaters which will mean that we have sent you 333
boxes altogether.

      We trust the sufferers will enjoy these Kippered Herrings
because they are grand quality and they are the identical same as we
supply to the Atlantic Liners.

      I caused a Fund to be started here in Aberdeen to help
these poor people and felt that sending them a few hundred boxes of
Kippered Herrings was doing them a good turn.   It was a terrible
calamity and we wish you every success in your endeavours to help
them.

             Yours faithfully,
             A. & M. Smith Limited.

                     H. A. Holmes.

                     Director.

And from Liverpool; 15 cases of Ham and Beef Roll, each case containing 72 tins, each tin containing 10 and a half ounces of the commodity." Another fish merchant, from Billingsgate in London sent a consignment of cured fish to be collected from Wrexham railway station.

Applications for Assistance from the Relief Fund.

The Gresford Disaster Relief Fund was designated to deal with relief for those affected by the Disaster. There was an immeasurable amount of form filling for all concerned, necessary, to ensure that monies were going to the right dependants and deserving cases. Letters such as these two from (an) anonymous source, (see copies of letters for comparison) did nothing to lessen the burden of those dealing with the Fund. There would always be those who thought they should 'have a piece of the cake', and although they were not entitled to relief, were jealous of others that were. Both these letters were undated,

Letter A. from 'A friend' to Mr E. D. Roberts (a Secretary) and the letter B from ' A miners wife' to Alderman C. O. Jones. The handwriting and spelling mistakes are so alike, that one suspects it was the same person who wrote both letters. Comparing the handwriting, it is difficult to judge whether the writer was male or female, as there were so many letters written in a similar style from both men and women. Here the writer alleges that the man named in the letters, (I have purposely omitted his name and address) received a weekly allowance through misrepresentation. (the spelling mistakes and grammar are those of the letter writer[s]: (see overleaf- letter A above)

Letter A.   *Just a line to inform you as if xxx of xxx is getting the Gresford Relief he is not intitled to it it is over two years since he work at Gresford. and if he is intilled to it thur is Plenty more as could do with it more than him. he gets Pencion for him and his wife and he has two big houses he tells People as they are Paid for he lives in one and gets 8/6 a week rent for the other he has no-one to keep. so he is neither in need nor intitled to it their is Plenty as worked thur after him. as is more in need: all the People is talking about it. it is two years in July since he last worked in Gresford. - from a friend.*

Letter B   *I am informing you as their is a man name xxx of xxx getting the relief of the Gresford and he as not worked in Gresford for over two years and he is not intilled to it and more so he is not in need of it him and his wife are getting old age Pencion and they have got two good houses. they get 8/6 for one and they live in the other they where telling People as he had retired from work: but when the Gresford fund started he went after it and had it, thur is menny. as worked thur after him and evant get it so how does he come in for it. he carnt denigh, as its two years since he went down Gresford Pit hoping he gets a stop to it he doesent fetch it until every man as had thurs. he is afraid of the men Pulling him up about it.   A miners wife*

The Secretaries and the Mayor of Wrexham were inundated with applications for relief from the Fund from every conceivable source, the 22nd (Cheshire) Regiment of Old Comrades' Association had also

To Mr E D Roberts — Gresford

Dear Sir Just a line to inform you as
if [name] ... ...
is getting the Gresford Relief he is not
intitled to it it is over two years since
he work at Gresford. and if he is
intitled to it their is Plenty more as
could do with it more than him. he
gets Pencion for him and his wife and
he has 2 big hours he tells People as they
are Paid for he lives in one. ang gets
8/6 a week rent for the other he has no one to
keep. so he is neither in need nor
intitled to it
their is Plenty as worked their after
him. as is more in need: all the People
is talking about it. it is two years in
July since he last worked in Gresford.
                    from a friend

Dear Sir.   Gresford.
                To Mr E J Jones. 3
I am informing you as their is a man
name
getting the relief of the Gresford and he is
not worked in Gresford for over two
years and he is not intolled to it and
more so he is not in need of it him
and his wife are getting old age Pencion
and they have got two good houses.
they get 8/6 for one and they live in
the other they where telling People as he
had retired from work: but when
the Gresford fund started he went
after it and had it, their is meny. as
worked their after him and cvant get
it so how does he come in for it. he
carnt denigh. as its two years since he
went down Gresford but hoping he
gets a stop to it he doesent fetch it.
untill every man as had theirs. he is
afraid of the men Pulling him up
about it.   a miners wife

received requests for help from men who had formerly served with them and who had been thrown out of work because of the Disaster. They requested information from the Secretaries as to what assistance the men would be entitled to in order to judge for themselves what assistance the Regiment should give.

The management at Wollaton Colliery in Nottingham, put forward the case of a young man who had been fatally injured at their mine by a roof fall, leaving a wife and six children, and asked, if there were any spare funds available, would the Secretaries consider this family.

A gentleman from the village of Rhosnessney on the outskirts of Wrexham wrote a personal letter to the Mayor of Wrexham Councillor Hampson on behalf of a widow in his village who had lost her husband a few weeks previously in an accident at Gresford Colliery. He asked if she could have a little help as in all probability had he lived, the family would have been affected by the disaster, and up to the time of writing she had not received any compensation. The scales of relief shows what unemployed men could expect to receive. The rules were strict, if you did not apply or fill in the forms, you would not get it as a matter of course, as many found out.

A man who had left the area to find work in St.Helens enquired;
I received word from home in which is in (Pandy) that men who as lost tools down Gresford are going to get £2 well I hope you don't forget about me for I was working with my Father from Feb 28th 1932 to the time of the Disaster Sept 22 1934, you will know my Father xxxx we worked in 29 district down the Dennis, well I hope you do your best for me for the Tools belonged to me and Dad.

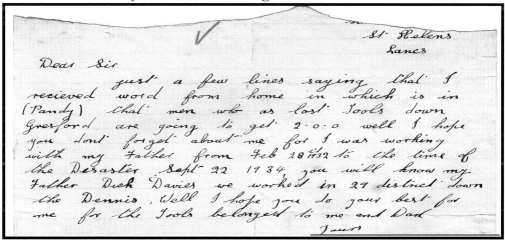

Some of the legitimate claims must have been difficult to read in view of the tragic circumstances of their request, - from a widow, this letter;

I'm making an application for extra money to get nourishment as I am not very strong. Losing my little girl make a big differant (sic) to my pay, I miss that for little extras. P.s. I also make a claim for funeral expences (sic), for my child who died March 3. I would like this matter settled too if possible as it is a long time for Mr Thomas (the funeral director) to wait for settlement.

Another form Rhosddu asked for help with the medication of the time for her child:-

Mr. H. W. Tomlinson,
6, Ashfield Rd,
Crispin Lane,
Rhosddu,

Dear Sir,

I am applying for nourishment for my baby, as he is very ill with pneumonia, the Doctor has told us to give him as much Brandy as possible and we are spending 16/4 per week, and I can't possibly keep it up,

this is what it takes, from Monday, to following Sunday,

1/3 Per Day Brandy,
10d. " " Linseed,
3d. " " Oil,

To Oblige,
H. W. Tomlinson

There were six survivors who were very lucky to have escaped and felt that grants from the Fund should have been more readily forthcoming in view of what they had endured. After writing several times since October 1934 they wrote once again on the 31st January 1935:

Gentlemen, We the six survivors of the Gresford disaster, do hearby appeal to you for a further grant as promised some time ago. We thank you ever so much for what you have done in the past on our behalf, We feel gentlemen having gone through such an ordeal that we require a little more to keep ourselfs fit, in the event of us being offered work either at Gresford or elsewhere, Having gone through such an ordeal we are still feeling the effects very acutly, (sic) And now we understand an attempt is to be made to decend (sic) the pit probably work will be resumed in the near future, Theirfore (sic) gentlemen we want to be ready and more so fit for such a task, Trusting our appeal will not be in vain.

They included with this letter, medical certificates from the doctors who recommended *"extra nourishment and a change of air, as they were suffering from a nervous disability caused by their ordeal in the Gresford disaster."*

The Secretaries also received very sad letters requesting assistance, but as the circumstances of their needs were not related to the Gresford disaster, there was nothing they could do to help, and more often than not, were unable to suggest where these people could apply elsewhere, for assistance. One ex-miner, for instance, included with his letter of application, a certificate from William Bonsall (the Gresford Colliery Manager) explaining that he had been employed at Gresford Colliery from 1926 to 1934 when they *"very reluctantly had to stop him, owing to having fits"*, and considered it very unsafe for him to be working underground. Another ex-miner who had been unemployed *"owing to the tence (sic) heat,"* eighteen months previously, put his case politely:

Sirs

Shall I appeal to you gentlemen of the Committee to allow me on small relief in the form of a grant just enough to purchase a change of Bedclothes and underwear for my wife and myself. My wife is on her sick bed very ill and has been for six months. I am afraid of the worst happening. What a sight it would be for anyone to see I am in receipt of 26/- dole 6/- rent 3/6 for coal Sirs I hope and trust the committee will consider our case, you have my word that you can make any inquiries you wish as better still anyone can pay me a visit. Dear Sirs Kindly grant one this request I want nothing further I shall esteem a great favour. If you wish one to visit you I will do with pleasure but give me a day in between for me to get someone in to look after my wife till I come back thanking you in every respect kindly accept the complements of the season.

The Secretaries would consider this ex-miner's application when he had furnished them with a certificate as to the last date he was on the Colliery books, unfortunately this showed that he had left the employment of Gresford Colliery in March 1933 therefore excluding him from the Relief Fund.

They were to receive many such letters that they were unable to deal with, including this very sad one from a man in South Wales:

I hope you will excuse me writing to you, I thought you might be able to help me. I was miner until 3 years ago when I had an accident which injured my spine I have been in bed since as I can't move anything below my hips I have to be changed 4 and 5 times a day owing to getting wet and I rots a lot of Bedclothes. I have been in hospital for 16 months and I have been home since I get some very bad pains 3 and 4 times a day, and I got to take at least 2 Morphia pills a day as the doctor says there is nothing else to do. But he told me to try and get a Motor carriage as I could go somewhere each day and see different things that might interest me I have a wicker carriage in which I was out in most of last summer but its rather heavy to push about and I did not go anywhere only in the street with it. So if you could help me in any way or advise me where I might be able to get help I would be very grateful. I am Married with wife and two children one 10 years the other just 12. I get £1.1.6 comp. and 10/-relief. So you see I am not begging for any money to live but just to be able to go out from my bed three or four days a week.

One of the Secretaries replied the next day:

I am sorry to understand that you have been so badly crippled and sincerely wish I was able to help you in obtaining a motor-carriage as you mention. The provisions in the Scheme, operating this Fund does not permit us to consider any application other than from the dependants of the victims of the disaster; neither do I know of any other agency to which you might apply.

The Fund Secretaries received many begging letters they could not assist with, and many strange ones that did not make sense. As any coal-mining disaster has repercussions further afield than the locality of the colliery, this one was no exception, as this man from Rhos, who had lost his livelihood because of the disaster, demonstrates. He was appealing to the committee for some sort of recompense:

I wonder whether your committee would consider my case which is singular but I think deserving. I run a workman's service from Rhos to Gresford Colliery. Last May I bought a Bus to take the place of the covered wagon to maintain this service. It cost me £95 to put her on the road and the licence and insurance is over £50 per annum. In addition to this I kept the lorry to carry workmen's coal and to do odd jobs. During this last three weeks the bus has been idle and owing to the workmen's coal being practically stopped the lorry is almost at a standstill. I am not getting any unemployment pay because I am not allowed to pay it. I have a wife and mother who is widowed to support and very little to support them with because it cost me 30/- per week approx to keep my motors on the road. Trusting that you will consider my case.

There have been many arguments and cause for complaint about how the Fund was managed and distributed, and the scale of payment was judged unfair by some, including the author of this letter, 29th March 1935:

With reference to publication in the Daily Herald of the above date I should like to know why are the scales of Widows and children only published and not the scales for the other Dependants since the outset of the fund nothing is said as regards Dependants Scales which is shameful is it because young men do not matter at all or is it the shame to publish so small an amount so that Public Opinion would be Roused. I want to know and get the Scales published for Every Dependant otherwise I am going to have the Public to see and know our treatment which is shameful as you know Mothers and Dependants are not state aided as the widows are.

Letters From Overseas.

The number of letters received by the Fund, from overseas, show how far and wide the news of the mining disaster at Gresford spread. Not only Europe, but as far afield as America, Australia and Canada, affecting, especially, those expatriates so far away from home. The Doyen of the Consular Corps and Consul for Uruguay, in Cardiff, was one of the first consuls to express their sympathy, and the 2nd Battalion of the Welch Fusiliers serving at Buena Vista Barracks in Gibraltar opened a subscription list hoping to send a cheque by the 12th October.
The Saint David's Welsh Society of Ottawa, Canada wrote on the 27th September expressing their sincere sympathy and:

were deeply shocked on reading the sad news in the papers here on Saturday last and followed keenly the later reports, hoping against hope that the number of lives lost would not be so heavy as at first reported. Our thoughts are with you in your sorrow, ... All our Welsh people living in Ottawa, and, we are sure, throughout Canada, are moved to sorrow for their brethren at home who are now undergoing so great an ordeal of suffering and bereavement.

Another Welsh Society, the Cymmrodorion Society of Sydney, Australia sent their sincere sympathy and a cheque for £16.7.9 on the 3rd December 1934 which merited a reply from the Secretaries ....

The wonderful response from the people of the Empire generally has made it possible for the bereaved and those thrown out of employment to be adequately cared for, and the widows and orphans of the deceased miners have now an assured source of income.

The Cambrian Society of Victoria sent a bank draft for £39.12.1 and the Sons of England Patriotic and Benevolent Society, from the Grand Lodge of Africa, in Johannesburg, sent a cable and 100 guineas followed by a letter of confirmation:

The members of the Sons of England Patriotic and Benevolent Society come from all parts of the Empire, many from Wales itself, and I am desired to express through you our very deep sympathy with all those families who suffered such tragic loss and bereavement.

Time Present and Time Past are both perhaps present in time future, and time future contained in time past.[63]

Of all the overseas letters that I have read, this one from Fred Ennis of North Queensland, written on Boxing Day, 1934, addressed to the Manager of Gresford Colliery, intrigued me the most. The writing is clear, tidy and literate, intimating a man of intelligence. As a writer, I began to conjure up all sorts of stories, all sorts of reasons why, a man of such obvious compassion and intelligence, should have chosen to live his life as he had, imagining a man, maybe in his late fifties or sixties, running away from.... something, - for he chose not to return to England but wanted to be *"where the British flag flies."* Someone like a character portrayed in the writing of Joseph Conrad's Heart of Darkness, Nostromo and Lord Jim, where there is always a testing of a man's character in conditions of extreme danger and difficulty. Unfortunately there is no other mention of this man, nor a reply, which I find very sad, as he appeared to want to help a woman and her family - then again, maybe this is only the romantic notion of this writer;

I am writing this on the Woolgar Goldfield some 100 miles North of Richmond with the temperature around 116 degrees in the shade, but I have been thinking hard and decided to address the letter to you.
I was born many years ago in the South of England, drifted as a boy to the South American coast, shipped across to China, spent a good few years in the Amar River country, drifted on again from town to town eventually reached Singapore. I had a longing to get where the British flag flies, so came across to Port Darwin, came here, and the present address is permanent, - I hope. I met a young Englishman recently, and he forwarded me some English papers, the first I had seen for years, and I read in one, of your terrible calamity and loss of life, as an Englishman a long way 'East of Suez' I felt deeply sorry for those who were taken away and the unfortunate families left. After such a long time away from civilization I feel I would like to hear once more again from the old Homeland; have someone there who would write and tell me the happenings of the day, send me papers, and different little things I might like sent along, and this is my object in writing to you and I trust you will understand.

I would like you to hand this letter on to a lady who has lost her breadwinner and has been left with young children and whose outlook is anything but bright, and who is prepared to write to me and forward along different odds and ends that will help me forget Satan's playground North of the Equator, and become really British once again. Just as soon as I hear from whoever will write me I will immediately reply and send sufficient money along for papers etc and will more than compensate her for whatever kindness bestowed on me, - to be frank I would like to help one family (in my own little humble way) until the dark clouds of trouble give way to sunshine. At present I am working a Gold show, by no means a Klondyke, and my nearest neighbour is ten miles away over rough country, and a feeling of loneliness sometimes creeps in, and papers and news from home would certainly cheer things up considerably. I sincerely hope you will do this for me and I will axiously (sic) await a letter from someone unknown.

Wishing England all prosperity in 1935. Fred Ennis

Women and Children.
    You don't know a woman until you have had a letter from her.[64]

It is difficult to find a suitable heading for these first two letters, nevertheless I feel that they should be included here as they concern two women asking about the bodies of their menfolk - the only letters, 'in the files,' from the relatives, on this subject.

To Mr Edward Jones (North Wales Miner's Office.)
Jan: 15th 1935.
    I am writing this letter to you to see if you could do anything towards hastening the decend (sic) of the Gresford pit. You will recall it is nearly four months since that terrible explosion happened and those bodies are still lying down that terrible pit. it makes me think that they are forgetting all about them, the shock may be over with some people but it is not over in my home. I feel sure a good many of those bodies are recognisable if they could only be got from there, we are holding out good hopes of having my brother's remains to bury ourselves, if they would only make a start and get the fan going, it would soon be safe enough for anyone to go down. if these experts are afraid why don't they open the pit and give the practical men a chance, you will find out that those bodies would be from their (sic) in a very short time while these experts are still dilly-dallying. Many think the time has come when the Mine Federation ought to demand those bodies. We have been waiting very patiently since the Inquiry passed at Xmas, when Sir Henry Walker remarked that his next job was to get down and recover the bodies. How much longer have we got to wait I earnestly appeal to you to try and do your best in that direction, we are all nearly broken-hearted with this terrible waiting.
Trusting you will do your best   Yours truly,

This second letter is written over a year after the disaster took place.
7.10.35
                 Dear Sir
I am writing to beg of you as Mother of one who was lost in the Gresford Colliery Disaster last September that you will make every possible effort to influence the Management and other officials concerned in the matter to try and recover the Body of my Son ? of ? I should be very grateful if you would on my behalf press the persons dealing with this matter to do their utmost to look for his Body and you would receive the Gratitude of an aged Mother.

School-children and Teachers.
We keep passing unseen through little moments of other people's lives.

Many schoolchildren were saddened to hear of the mining disaster at Gresford and were prompted to send donations in aid of the children left behind. A reader may not believe that people, especially children, could be affected by something that did not concern them. This may well have been the case, but the children, whose letters I am using here, were touched in some way, whether it was because they themselves came from mining areas, or their school teacher was Welsh or there was a 'Welsh connection.' As a child growing up in the Sixties I was extremely saddened by the Aberfan Disaster. My 'connectedness' was that I had not long left junior school, I had recently been to Wales on a family holiday and my teacher, Mr Jones was a Welshman. I am reminded of the old adage, that everyone remembers where they were when J. F. Kennedy was shot, I don't, but I do remember where I was, and what I was doing when the Aberfan Disaster happened. All those children from Aberfan touched my life, then as a child, and as an adult now living in Wales, they touch me still. Carrying out this research has meant that my life has been 'touched again' by another 'coal related' disaster.

There were letters from a mining village in Derbyshire whose children are *"therefore fully alive to the dangers which constantly attend employment in the mine"*, and Sowerby Bridge where the children live near a coalfield and *" know some little of your sad hearts,"* and from Sunderland;
"Your tragic loss has touched our hearts. The agony of the women who waited at the pithead was shared by us, for we too live in a mining area." From Rhiwlas near Bangor, North Wales a headmaster forwarded donations from a fund he had instigated which included money from *"quarrymen who are already contributing through their Union and many farmers who had already been approached at the sales."*

From the Mantle Road Girl's School in Leicester the following letters were sent to the Mayor. The headmistress enclosed a cheque for £5 and the sympathy of the staff and scholars, two of which, wrote their own letters on behalf of the school and friends:

My schoolfellows, teachers and myself have much pleasure in sending you the enclosed cheque for five pounds, to help in alleviating the suffering caused by the Gresford Colliery Disaster. We all realise what a terrible ordeal the dependents must be going through, and hope that our small token of sympathy will help to bridge it over and make at least some of their lives brighter and more comfortable. I remain, Yours truly, E. W.

My classmates and I would like to show our deepest sympathy in the terrible disaster that has just occurred and has turned the peaceful little town of Gresford into a state of chaos. I was shocked and dismayed to hear of the tragic occurrence and I hope that never again will such a thing happen. We have contributed a small sum each and have got together a sum of five pounds, which has been enclosed with this letter together with my deepest sympathy. I remain Yours truly, A.D.

Adoption

As mentioned, the initial report that came from the office of the Lord Lieutenant and made in a broadcast to the nation by the Acting Lord Mayor of London, Sir Louis Newton, that the explosion at Gresford Colliery had left 800 fatherless children, was an incorrect one. In the first month after the disaster, the offices of the Secretaries were inundated with enquiries regarding the adoption or care of these "fatherless children." What appears to have been lost in consideration, is the fact that a) Of the 241 fatherless children, the majority still had a Mother to look after them; being fatherless did not make them necessarily Motherless too and, b) the highlighting - focusing attention on, one individual child who had been left an orphan on the death of her father, did not mean that all the other fatherless children were orphans too. This naming of an individual child meant that many people applied to adopt one little child 'in particular'.

Offers to adopt or care for the "orphans" came from individuals, families, and institutions such as convents, orphanages and schools. I have mixed feelings about some of the offers made, not that they were necessarily disingenuous in their offer to help the children but I do question for whose benefit, the adoption was intended. For instance, a single woman writing from Devon on the 28th September asked whether there was a little girl of about ten years of age who had been orphaned in the disaster, whom she could "take and educate." She had just finished "educating one from the Rhondda valley" who had left her to train as a nurse, and as she was all alone would be glad of another child for company. The Mayor replied that her letter would "be passed to the proper quarter for attention."

On the 26th October she asked that she be put in touch with those who *"had the administration of the Relief Fund,"* and in return she was informed that her letter had been forwarded to Major Roberts (one of the Secretaries of the Relief Fund) and, *"we understand that a Committee are considering your very kind offer amongst numerous others which they have received, and no doubt they will be communicating with you at the earliest possible moment."* On the 13th of November she enquired:

I wrote about six weeks ago offering to take a little girl who had lost her father in the Gresford Mine explosion, and educate her. I stipulated that she should be about 10 years old, but I have been wondering as I have not heard from you, whether there was difficulty in finding a child of the right age, I do not really mind how young the child is so long as she is able to do some things for herself and I suppose she would have to travel here alone. She would be a long way from her friends so I suppose it would be better if she were motherless also, if there is a poor little thing like that, then I could take charge of her altogether.

A reply to this letter was not forthcoming, which may be one of the reasons she was prompted to write the following on the 15th January, 1935;

Judging from the reports in the paper, my offer to adopt a child whose father was killed in the Gresford Mine is entirely unnecessary. As my own circumstances have changed somewhat since I made my offer I should be glad to withdraw it.

An offer of a different kind, was sent within the first few days of the disaster, from an electrician in Surrey to the Editor of the Daily Herald:

I think there must be many cases where some poor distracted widows would be glad to have one or more of their children well looked after for a while until they have chance to collect themselves and make plans for the future. I am an electrician by trade (thank God regularly employed) with three children of my own. My wife and I would be very pleased to take one of these little mites, preferably a little girl 6 to 8 years of age to feed and clothe until her poor mother wanted her back. Now I have a suggestion that I should be grateful if you would publish. There are no doubt dozens of Labour men and women round London and suburbs in fact in all parts of the country who would be pleased to do the same but could not at a moments notice put down the money for the child's fare. Now in view of the considerable revenue the Railway Co's receive from or through the mining industry apart from the sympathy that no doubt exists in the minds of the Director's towards these poor little orphaned mites, I wonder if it could be possible for free vouchers to be issued..

From Essex, a poultry farmer writes in an unusual manner to 'adopt':

Dear Sirs and Mesdames

A childless and lonely couple of advanced middle age is desirous of meeting a girl about 14/15 years with a view to adoption, and wondering if you have such a person under your care. It is essential that the little lady we are looking for shall be entirely orphan, because she cannot have two homes. If she has been unhappy so much the better. She must be reasonably intelligent and bright, affectionate and lovable, and not ungainly. The girl would be required to share the work of the house with Mrs J (his wife) on the basis of a paid helper until we found out whether there was mutual attraction, and either way she would be treated with ungrudging generosity and consideration. As the girl we are enquiring for is likely to be in very poor circumstances, we venture to say that lack of outfit need be no deterrent we will see to that. Also any expenses this enquiry may involve will be very gladly met. The news of your terrible disaster was the first which greeted us upon our return from a holiday trip to Madeira and the Canary Islands, and as my wife lost her own father in the Staffordshire mines when she was a motherless child of 5, you can easily understand how our hearts went out in sympathy..........

Many of the women who wanted to adopt had other children and wanted playmates for them, others had children who were grown and felt they would like to have another young family to lavish their love and attention on, while some women obviously wanted help around the house, assistance in their businesses and /or companionship.

Individuals and families.

One of the first letters received regarding adoption was this one addressed to the Mayoress written the day after the disaster from J Binns of Smethwick.: (see opposite)

We are very sorry to hear of the disaster at the Gresford Colliery today, we saw the account of it in the Sunday Pictorial, and that the Lord Marshall is willing to take three orphans. We also are willing to take one little girl about 7 years of age if you would find us one. We are in a good position to keep her and give her a good home and every comfort. My husband and I hope that you will give this letter your kind consideration and find us a nice little girl to adopt. Also please find enclosed a small donation of 2/6d.

Many women were moved to offer homes to the 'orphans' rather than think of them in an orphanage, the following letters highlights the naivety of those who assumed that what they heard or read was true and that they were the only ones to respond: - Mrs F. A. to the Acting Lord Mayor of London, after his radio broadcast to the nation, 28th September 1934:

I am writing to you as I believe you can help me on what I am about to

86 Reynolds St
Smethwick
Sept 23rd 1934

No J Binns

Dear Madam

We are very sorry to hear of the disaster at the Gresford Colliery to day, we saw the account of it in the Sunday Pictorial, and that Lord Marshall is willing to take to 3 Orphans, we also are willing to take to one little girl about 7 years of age, if you would find us one, we are in a good position to keep her. and give her a good home and every comfort.

my Husband and I hope that you will give this liddu your kind consideration and find us a nice little girl to adopt also please find Enclosed small Donation 2" 6 toward the fund.

We Remain yours Truly
mr & mrs Linden

write. It is so little one can do to help in such a disaster, but what I want to know is could I adopt that little girl of five years of age, she lost her father who was a widower, in the dreadful Gresford mine disaster. I have two sons, one who is 24 years of age as is serving in His Majesty's Navy and is at present in China, the other boy is nearly 16 years and will soon be thinking of leaving school and either going to business or follow his brother in the Navy. So we wondered if you would help us to adopt a little girl from Gresford the one I mention in particular. We have lived in this same house for over 30 years, and my Husband has been in his business place for 42 years. If you wish you can send for further particulars if you think there is any chance of me adopting a little girl. Please find enclosed 10/- postal order for the Lord Mayor's Distress Fund for dependants of Gresford Miners.

On the 9th October the husband wrote to the Mayor of Wrexham explaining that his wife had written with regard to adoption and he reiterated their family position and added the following:

I am almost 60 and my wife almost 46, we live in our own house in North London. We are of course purely British stock on both sides. We shall be pleased to hear the result of this application at an early date so that if successful, she may begin to make the necessary preparation for her reception and future life with us..

The Secretaries acknowledged the letter the next day and assured him that the matter would be placed before the Committee at the earliest opportunity and thanked him for his kindly interest in the *"little girl's future welfare."* A week later Mrs F. A. addressed herself to the wife of the Mayor of Wrexham repeating her offer:

I trust I am not going to be disappointed, only in yesterday's 'Daily Express' I noticed that the pensions for the dependants had been made out I only hope it doesn't mean I can't have the little girl. We simply want to adopt her, her pension could be shared amongst other unfortunates.........so we thought it would give us another interest in life to adopt the little girl. Since writing to the Lord Mayor of London I have been making little articles in the hopes I should hear we could adopt her and I was hoping I could have her soon to get her here and settled before we have our Xmas party. You will make me very happy if you write and say I can have her...... I sincerely hope I am not going to be disappointed after all my efforts.

The Lady Mayoress' reply of 27th October; *"..unfortunately with such a lot of work on hand, it is very difficult to get in touch with such a case. I will, however, forward your letter to the Joint Hon. Secretaries of the Fund, who may be able to let you know something definite within the next week or so."* Mrs F.A. wrote a fortnight later:

I am very anxious to know when I shall be having the little girl of 5 years, who is without Father and Mother. You will remember I wrote you before also Mrs Hampson the Lady Mayoress and said the Joint Secretaries would settle the question and let me know shortly. The letter I had from you was dated 11th Oct: and the one from the Mayoress 27th Oct: I do so hope we are not going to be disappointed as I have been making little necessarys and getting things ready for her for Xmas, we are so looking forward to having her. We wanted her to be here and settled in new surroundings before Xmas, as we always have a few little one's here for Xmas .... Could she not be sent by some of your people travelling to London and either brought to us here, or we could meet her from someone. Trusting we shall hear she is coming along.

Ten days later Mrs F.A. wrote again expressing her earnest wish to have the child, soon:

I hope you will excuse the liberty I take in writing to you again in regard to adopting the little girl of 5 years of age. Time is speeding along towards Xmas and we did hope to have her here and settled down before Xmas was too near. I trust my offer is not unsatisfactory and that I shall hear from you very soon to say she is coming. I have not given up hope, I am still making her some new clothes also getting her some things in for her share in our Xmas tree, which we always have for some less fortunate friends who have some young families. Though my own Sons are grown up we enjoy doing it for others. It is a long time since I wrote to you, 9th Oct: and time goes along so quickly, that I am hoping and trusting we are not going to be disappointed in my offer, and I do sincerely hope I shall have a letter from you to say we can expect her.

The Secretaries acknowledged her letter the next day stressing that the Committee would be unable to give a definite answer prior to the New Year, she wrote on the 18th December and impatiently, she wrote again on the 8th January, 1935:

Again I write you on behalf of the little girl we wished to adopt. A week has gone from the New Year, and now I hope your Committee have found it possible to settle the affair of adoption. We are thinking of settling our Easter holidays and wish to know how many of us will be going and if I shall be able to include the little girl in question.... P.S. If they cannot give me a definite answer, one way or another, and they still wish to consider it, they had better count me out, and then I can enquire elsewhere for a wee child who wants a home, there are many.

A week later, her last attempt:

.... I am still wishing to adopt her and you have my previous letters, and the New Year is well on the way so perhaps you could see into this matter at once for me, or put me in touch with the adoption committee........ So after all these months of trying to do a good turn I shall hear and succeed.

To which the Secretaries replied on the 19th February, 1935:

We have to acknowledge receipt of your letter of the 16th instant which is filed for attention in due course.

Mrs F.A. was not the only person who believed that adoption was a mere formality and that a child would be hers for the asking, Mrs O.M. of Tamworth also wrote several letters to the Mayor of Wrexham and the Secretaries expecting to be allowed to adopt a child. A widow from Colwyn Bay advised the Secretaries that she wanted an orphan child and should also require full particulars as to the respectability of the family:

I should want the child for three months before legalising and deciding whether I should adopt it.

From Derbyshire a married lady schoolteacher asked,

"Can I offer a home to one of the children belonging to a stricken family? I should like a girl between seven and eleven if the mother could spare her to me."

This schoolteacher offered a good home and education to a *"fairly intelligent child"* so that there would be *"some chance of training her for the teaching profession"* She wished to get the child away from the effects of the terrible calamity and, of course, *" the adoption of the child will be my ultimate desire although I should not wish her to forget her family."*

Via the Mayor of Blackburn came a request from a woman in his own town who was in *"delicate health"*, wanting an older child *"of the Catholic faith."* Maybe because the Secretaries were not able to deal with the matter until the New Year, and it had taken them two months to reply to her original letter, she wrote on the 30th December; *"I have been able to get one elsewhere so shall not trouble you in the matter further."*

Children's Societies, Orphanages and Schools.

Offers from various societies dealing with the care and education of children, along with offers from individuals to *"take and educate"* the *"orphans of Gresford"*, flooded in from all parts of the country, many within the first month after the disaster. The inaccurate report that there were 800 fatherless children meant that people thought there were 800 potential orphans to adopt and educate. What sort of checks were made as to the suitability of the intended carer and educator, whether individual or establishment? The compatibility, home background and mental stability of the child, seemed more important than their actual well-being and happiness. As with the matter of adoption, I question for whose benefit, these offers were made, and the motivation behind the offers. In the newspapers, advertisements for various adoption societies and schools were 'strategically' placed next to the reports of the Gresford Disaster and the subsequent inquiry - Why? Was this a recruitment drive on behalf of the Homes? Had they read that there would be a Relief Fund, so would be assured of their fees if they took in any of these "orphans"?

I was at once, both moved and irritated reading the dispassionate letters from the various organisations, irritated by what appeared to be a condescending and patronising attitude on the part of the adults who wanted to 'help' and moved when thinking about the children, their grief and all the emotions of losing a parent and the strangeness of the situation. Living in an area of North Wales, in the 1990's, that had seen and heard the details of one of the longest running child abuse inquiries this century; and listening and reading of inquiries into abuse of children in different homes, countrywide, going back to the 1930's and 1940's, I was guilty of "presumptive thinking" without knowing the full facts. I have asked questions that remain unanswered, I have searched through the documentary evidence in the hope of finding answers, yet have come to realise that there will always be something "missing or misplaced."
Documentary evidence relating to the Gresford Disaster is still "waiting to be catalogued," all, missing pieces of the Gresford Disaster "Jigsaw". By sifting and sharing the evidence that is available, i.e. the letters, we can maybe find and add to, not only the "Gresford jigsaw", but other "jigsaws" too.

A school in Birmingham offered two or three vacancies for children whose mother or father may have formerly lived in the Birmingham area:
*Boarding Foundationers shall be children of good character and sufficient health who by reason of orphanage or other special adversity shall in the opinion of the Governors be **proper objects of bounty**, and whose parents are, or if dead, were inhabitants of the City of Birmingham. No boy or girl shall be admitted to the school under the age of nine years.*

The Smith Orphan Homes in West Yorkshire also offered places to those children with a connection to Yorkshire. Six months later, 17th April 1935, the Secretary Superintendent of the Smith home was prompted to write again after reading a report in the newspaper that others were still making offers to care for some of the fatherless children, this time from Australia:
..I see in today's issue of the London Daily Telegraph that Fairbridge Farm School is prepared to accept fifty children who have been left

orphan and fatherless as a result of the Gresford Mining Disaster. My Board of Management will be happy to render help to your committee on behalf of any boy or girl who stands in need, now or in the future. The enclosure may be of interest to you and I would respectfully draw your attention to the last pages, headed " Special Benefits." I may say that these Homes are an endowed charity responsible to H.M. Board of Education and the Charity Commissioners

Prompted by the same news report, but this time in the Daily Express, the Borough Treasurer of Manchester wrote a personal recommendation for the Fairbridge Farm School, Australia:

I read in the Daily Express about your Gresford boys who contemplate going to Westralia,(Western Australia) they could not do better....... a son of a friend of his was "going about Australia" , reporting for a Home Society in England and had paid a visit to one of the Fairbridge Farm Schools reporting in "very eulogistic terms." He urged them to let the boys go so as not "to be tied to their mother's apron strings," and that they would soon be able to send for the rest of the family.

This information was incorrect, as the Fairbridge Farm Schools in Australia, as well as in New Zealand and Rhodesia, were formed to keep and train young men and women, and eventually help them to find employment in the farming industry. The ultimate aim, of course, was to increase the population of the respective countries after the heavy loss of lives in the 1st World War.[65]

The Secretary and Collector of the Cherrytree Orphanage, was instructed to express the sympathy of his Committee and offer accommodation to girl orphans between the ages of five and ten, and wrote to the Management of Gresford Colliery:

...Before the admittance of the children we should desire the opportunity of coming over to see them, as of course, we wish to keep up the present high standard of the children in the Orphanage.

The National Children's Home and Orphanage were prepared to offer facilities to: *children of all Christian denominations, except Roman Catholics, for whom their own Church authorities wish to make provision.*

The Chief Organising Secretary of The National Farthing League, in aid of Dr. Barnardo's Homes. whose motto was **No Destitute Child Ever Refused Admission** informed the Management of Gresford Colliery that the Homes had *"despatched agents to Gresford immediately to offer admission to all children left destitute."*

The wonderfully named John Grooms Crippleage and Flower Girls Mission from Middlesex offered to help.

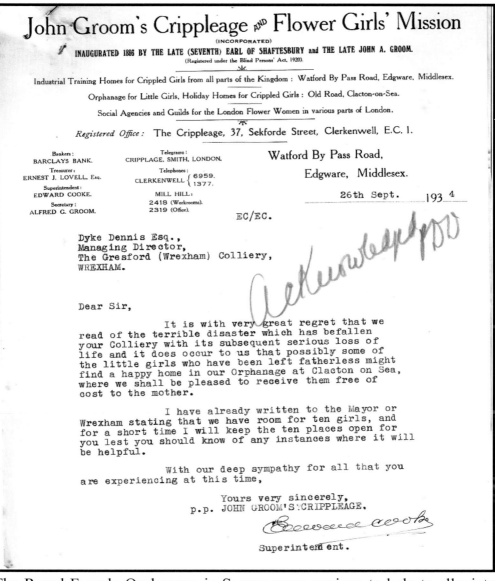

The Royal Female Orphanage in Surrey were anxious to help to alleviate the distress and offered: *early admission, without election, to any girl or girls between the ages of 7 and 12. From admission until 16 they will be educated, maintained and trained, and then found a good situation and given a good start in life. We already have miner's children from South Wales and Durham, all of whom are doing well, and we are ready to help you at once should it be necessary.*

The Superintendent of The Spurgeon's Orphan Homes contacted the vicar of the Baptist Church in Wrexham with an offer to *"take a considerable number of fatherless boys,"* and that, *"no votes were required to secure admission to these Homes, the greatest need is the loudest voice."* The letter was passed on to the Secretaries who decided to *"give due publicity to the kind offer,"* and would write if they had any applications.

An offer to admit children, *" until such time as they could complete their education, were self - supporting or able to return to their homes,"* came from The Shaftesbury Homes and *"Arethusa"* Training Ship which was a caring, rather than an adoptive society, The Training Ship provided vacancies for boys of *"sound physique etc. who wish(ed) to go to sea and were between the ages of 13 and a half and 15."*

The Sisters of Charity from the St. Agnes' Home, for 50 girls, would be: very glad to adopt one little girl of nine or ten years old,
....She should be a child of normal health and intelligence, as we are only certified for such children, and I shall have to ask for a medical certificate to be filled in, and she will have to pass our own doctor. On hearing from you that you will accept our offer, I will send you the necessary forms. We can arrange to have the child sent off from Chester in the Bristol train, and we will take her and bring her up free of all charge, and start her well in life. I think I can promise you that she will be happy with us.
For some reason this letter did not receive a reply until the 14th December, by which time the offer had expired:
I had quite given up all hope of receiving a reply to my offer, it is so long since I made it. You will understand that it means a good deal to us to take free children, and we cannot keep the matter open indefinitely. We have accepted others since I made the offer to you, and I must therefore say now that we are obliged to withdraw it.

The Editor of the Daily Mirror received a letter from the Founder and Secretary of the Heritage Craft Schools, Hospitals and Homes for Cripples, Mrs C W K. CBE on the 1st October, 1934:
You will remember that at Chailey we have, as one of our proudest possessions, the Princess Elizabeth Clinic for Tiny Babes, and Mirror Grange - and I am wondering whether, in view of this grave Mine disaster in Wales, we can help by taking in any of the children temporarily, to be paid for by your relief fund. We happen to have a few vacancies on the boys' side, and if you think well of the suggestion, we could go into all details.

116

And also in the Daily Mirror (handwritten):

The crippled children have forestalled me in one way, for I understand they are making a collection of their pennies - very rare possessions – as they want to contribute towards the relief of the disaster, so I hope that the most will be made of these children's pennies. This I think should be held up as an example to charitably minded people. But in the meantime, I would go one step further and say that if you like to consider the possibility of sending some children here, and thus helping to distract the fatherless children for a while, we shall only be too happy to help to the best of our ability, and details as to numbers could be discussed if you think well of my suggestion. At any rate, I should like it to be known that we want to help. Charitably minded persons might be willing to pay for the children here, and the cost per child per week would be £1: 10: 0.

Mrs C W K. CBE. was instructed that her letter had been forwarded to the Mayor of Wrexham, to whom she wrote the following day:

The Daily Mirror tell me they have sent a letter I wrote to them on to you for I understand I should have written to you direct in the matter. The fact remains that if at these Heritage Craft Schools we can take in any of these unhappy children who have been bereaved by father or relatives, we shall be happy to do so provided you can pay for them out of your relief fund. The spirit of our letter is that in which an armless boy has written when sending a donation to the relief fund, namely that of a great desire to help if possible in any way in connection with this terrible disaster. I may add that we have Babes from the youngest possible age and that our schools are for both sexes. I think my suggestion may be a helpful one, as in the days of the Great War when we found that one of the best means of helping was to remove children from raid-shock areas to these happy surroundings at Chailey, where they were able to forget the terrors of the raids, etc. Our children at the heritage are paid for at the rate of £92 per annum, but we should be only too willing to reduce this to 35/- per week or even 30/- per week under these circumstances. We have a delightful home at the seaside, which would be a great change for the children, as well as these Schools in the heart of Sussex.

The Joint Secretaries sent this reply;

Dear Madam

Your letter of the first instant addressed to The Editor, Daily Mirror, has been forwarded to us. We note what you say relative to your offer to help by taking in any of the children temporarily to be paid for by the relief fund, and we will take an early opportunity of placing your letter before the appropriate Committee who has this part of the work in hand, and who, no doubt, will communicate with you on the subject in due course.

It is wonderfully good of the little children to be making a collection of their pennies towards the fund, and on behalf of the Relief Committee may we take this opportunity through you of expressing their deep sense of gratitude.

It is difficult to understand the motive of Mrs C.W.K. without being uncharitable. On the surface it appears that this woman was using her position to further the cause of the Orphanage she was associated with. As a business woman she would have been aware of the money available from a Relief Fund for any dependants and she was not offering any free places only a small reduction on fees payable.

To take and train young girls.

While many places such as The Pensarn Private Domestic Training Establishment were prepared to take immediate care of children, (in this case at a cost of 15/- per week, for which money from the Relief Fund was expected to be allocated) to train for domestic work of all kinds, the majority of the offers of work for young girls, as 'domestic help', came from the private household. Some of the requests for 'girl help' or 'maid servant' were very particular about the sort of person they were prepared to employ. Requests such as these were all too familiar, well intentioned they may have been, yet shown to be extremely prejudicial. This letter addressed to the Mayor of Wrexham outlines the particular attributes required by a lady of a girl applying to her for employment:

Knowing that you are in touch with the relatives of the victims of the terrible Gresford Colliery accident I am taking the liberty of writing to you. I am looking for a young girl as a domestic servant and have been thinking you may know of some young girls who will have to earn their own living and would like this kind of work. Experience is not necessary as I am willing to train a young girl providing she is:

1. Of good character.
2. Of clean and neat appearance
3. Strong and healthy.
4. Fond of children.
5. Not too short - say about 5ft 4ins.
6. Willing to work and be trained.
7. Young, steady and likely to settle down in my home.
I do not wish to employ a Roman Catholic would like Church of England if possible, also the girl must not be afflicted with cast on eye, stammering or deafness. I state this because I have a small daughter age 3yrs. I shall be very much obliged if you would give my name and address to any girls whom you may think suitable.

118

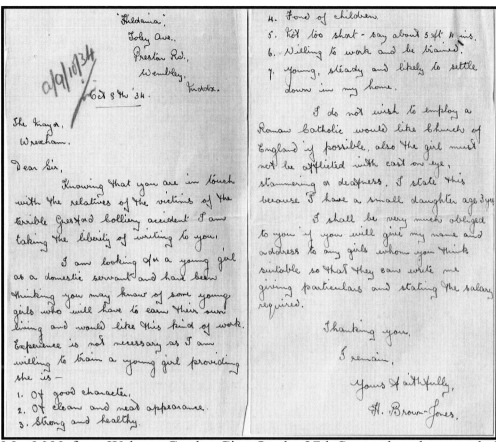

"Hildania",
Tolsy Ave.,
Preston Rd.,
Wembley,
Middx.
Oct 8th '34.

9/10/34

The Mayor,
Wrexham.

Dear Sir,

Knowing that you are in touch with the relatives of the victims of the terrible Gresford Colliery accident I am taking the liberty of writing to you.

I am looking for a young girl as a domestic servant and have been thinking you may know of some young girls who will have to earn their own living and would like this kind of work. Experience is not necessary as I am willing to train a young girl providing she is —

1. Of good character.
2. Of clean and neat appearance.
3. Strong and healthy.
4. Fond of children.
5. Not too short - say about 5 ft 4 ins.
6. Willing to work and be trained.
7. Young, steady and likely to settle down in my home.

I do not wish to employ a Roman Catholic would like Church of England if possible, also the girl must not be afflicted with cast in eye, stammering or deafness. I state this because I have a small daughter age 3 yrs

I shall be very much obliged to you if you will give my name and address to any girls whom you think suitable so that they can write me giving particulars and stating the salary required.

Thanking you,

I remain,

Yours faithfully,

H. Brown-Jones.

Mrs.M.N. from Welwyn Garden City. On the 27th September she appealed for:

any likely girls who would like to come and work for her, to write to her direct and they would find that "life in her house was much easier than in other houses." On the 17th October she "hoped they would soon be able to give publicity to her request; It is now three weeks since I wrote and I cannot of course keep the offer open indefinitely. I have been holding up other enquiries till I should hear something definite from Wrexham. I thought one mother might be thankful to know her daughter was in a good home, where good food and kind treatment would not be lacking." (see overleaf)

On the 3rd November 1934 she wrote again:

With further reference to my previous letters, I am rather surprised I have heard nothing further from you. I should have thought there must be someone in touch with the homes of these unfortunate people. I also understand that Welsh girls were only too glad of a chance to find work, but apparently I was mistaken. I at least expected you would have acknowledged receipt of the clothing I sent you, even if you could not help me in the other matter.

"THE SHANTY,"
9, BARLEY CROFT GREEN,
WELWYN GARDEN CITY,
HERTS.

Dear Sirs,

I have to thank you for your letter of the 29th. ult.

I hope you will soon be able to give publicity to my request. It is now three weeks since I wrote & I cannot of course keep the offer open indefinitely. I have been holding up other enquiries till I should hear something definite from Wrexham. I thought one mother might be thankful to know her daughter was in a good home, where good food & kind treatment would not be lacking.

I have already made my contribution towards the Lord Mayor's fund, but I am sending under separate cover (today) a parcel of warm clothing, which I think may be useful.

I hope you will let me know if you have been able to get into touch with any likely girls.

Thanking you.

Yours faithfully

(Mrs). M. B. North.

"THE SHANTY,"
9, BARLEY CROFT GREEN,
WELWYN GARDEN CITY,
HERTS.

Dear Sirs,

With further reference to my previous letters, I am rather surprised I have heard nothing further from you. I should have thought there must be some one in touch with the homes of these unfortunate people. I also understood that Welsh girls were only too glad of the chance to find work, but apparently I was.

mistaken.

I, at least, expected you would have acknowledged receipt of the clothing I sent you, even if you could not have helped me in the other matter.

Yours faithfully,

(Mrs) M.B. North.

To "take and educate" boys.

An exchange of letters from C.R. of Kensington concerning his offer to be responsible for the education of one or two boys at his Preparatory School, went on for nearly eight months. On the 3rd November, 1934 the Joint Secretaries wrote to C.R. thanking him for a letter that had been forwarded to them, from the Managing Director of Gresford Colliery, Mr. Henry Dyke Dennis on the 27th September, 1934

We desire to express to you our sincere regret at the delay in dealing with this matter, but the Committee decided, having regard to the number of similar generous offers, to appoint a Committee to deal with this matter generally. The Committee will have the assistance, it is hoped, of His Majesty's, Inspector of Schools and Directors of Education. I am sure you will appreciate that up to now the Committee has been extremely busy in dealing with individual cases of immediate distress, and the delay in dealing with your letter has not been due to any overlooking of your very kind and sympathetic action in this matter, for which we are asked to convey to you the grateful thanks of the Lord Lieutenant and the Committee. We may add that Mr Dennis takes a personal interest in all communications sent to him relating to the relief and assistance of those involved in this terrible disaster.

5th November. C.R. letter to Secretaries, headed Educational Help for boys;

Many thanks for your very courteous letter of the 3rd instant relative to my offer in connection with the above. I fully appreciate all you say and how much your time must have been occupied in dealing with those immediate demands, but when these have been disposed of if it is then found possible to avail yourself of what I have suggested, I can assure you it will be a privilege to do what I can to assist and shall be happy to cooperate with you to the fullest extent in my power to that end. I shall look forward to hearing from you later and you may rest assured of my very hearty cooperation and sympathetic help.

On the 7th November the Secretaries thanked him for his letter, noting the contents.

C.R. to the Secretaries on the 5th December, Education of Boys.

Referring to exchange of letters hereon, has this matter been able to receive further investigation yet, if not, can you say when it will be possible to do so.

On the 19th December, C.R. wrote again, Educational Help for boys.

Further to our exchanged correspondence hereon, I shall be glad to know at your kind convenience, if it has been found possible to give this suggestion further and more definite consideration, and if so whether you have any boys in mind who you would wish to send here for interview and examination on the lines indicated in my previous letters, if so, the School Christmas Vacation would afford a good opportunity to make such arrangements, and upon receipt of the necessary details relative to such applicants I will go into the matter further. Be assured of all my help to meet such cases as may present themselves.

5th January 1935, C.R. to the Secretaries. Education of boys.

Referring to our exchanged letters hereon, I shall be glad to know if you are now able to report progress and if there is any likelihood in the near future of my being able to interview and examine any such boys as you desire to take advantage of my offer.

12th January, C.R. to the Secretaries. Education of boys.
Further to this matter and our exchanged letters hereon, especially that of yours of the 3rd November last, can you yet inform me if any steps have been or will be taken in respect to the offer I have made by the Committee that has been set up and if as an educationist and psychologist of wide experience I can be of any general help to that Committee I shall be happy to do so.

19th January, C.R. again, this time to H. Dyke Dennis. Gresford Colliery Disaster. Education of Boys.
Further to our exchanged letters hereon, apart from an acknowledging letter of the 3rd NOVEMBER last from the Secretaries to the Relief Committee, I have been quite unable to elicit any further information as to whether or not I can be of assistance in the direction I have previously offered, and must be pardoned if I both regret such apathy and asked to be excused from writing further - I have written them four times since without acknowledgement. I am nevertheless still open to help if I can.

22nd January, Henry Dyke Dennis to Major R. Roberts, Chief Secretary to the Relief Fund;
I enclose a copy of a letter from Mr. C.R, I really think the Committee should answer his letter seeing that he has been most kind in offering to take these boys, and the least they could do is to tell him what they want. Will you kindly see to this matter.

Mr Roberts replied directly to C.R. on the 24th January:
Gresford Colliery Disaster.
Mr Dennis has forwarded to me copy of your letter to him of the 19th January. The Committee very much regret the delay in dealing with this matter. We would like to point out that before any selection can be made of the children many enquiries have to be made as to the suitability of the children, the consent of the parents, reports on the educational advancement of the children, and others of a similar kind. The formation of a Central Board to deal with the Fund will be shortly effected, and its local administration Committee also appointed. Until this Committee and the Central Board are in existence there is no authority to make definite

decisions in cases requiring special consideration, and whilst the Committee desire to reiterate their very grateful thanks to you for your most generous offer we would ask you to bear with us for a short time, having regard to the fact that the staff dealing with this Fund is purely voluntary, and the case requiring attention are extremely numerous. We assure you no discourtesy was intended.

Having received this explanation as to why he had not heard from the Secretaries he replied:

Education of Boys. 25th January 1935.

I am in receipt of your letter of yesterday hereon and note contents with thanks. I fully appreciate your many difficulties. You may rest well assured that the thought of any sort of intentional discourtesy did not enter my mind, all I was anxious about was that the offer at any rate might not be lost sight of. As I have said, if I can assist further in this important and by no means easy educational side of the future of those boys so seriously affected and the enquiries or investigations which are admittedly essential, I am yours to command.

The Secretaries were obviously still busy elsewhere, and C.R. having read in the press that the *"Scheme of Distribution had been determined and agreed"* asked on the 16th February

I hope it may be possible to advance this suggestion of mine to a practical end at any rate to the extent of being able to interview and examine any boys that may be suitable.

and again on the 3rd March,

Gentlemen, Gresford Colliery Disaster. Education of boys.

Further to the above I am still without any definite reply from you on this matter and must really ask after all this time if you have any intention of taking advantage of the offer I made and if so when I first wrote on the 26th September last.

On the 9th March C. R. wrote two letters, one to the Secretaries,

Sirs, Colliery Disaster Fund. Education of boys.

Referring to my many communications hereon, as it appears quite impossible to get anything definite on this question or to arrive at any helpful understanding or progress I am unable to keep my offer open any longer unless I am assured of something definite in the immediately near future. I have done my best but it seems to meet with no response.

and the other to Mr. Henry Dyke Dennis.

My dear Sir.
Gresford Colliery Disaster. Education of boys.
With reference to your kindly interest in my offer in connection with the above, it is with the utmost reluctance that I have to say that it being apparently impossible to get this matter to a stage of even approaching any decision and having heard nothing whatever from the Secretaries for the past two months and other letters from me since having been simply ignore I have informed them - the Secretaries - today that I cannot continue my offer any longer unless there is some indication that it is in some way likely to meet with a definite response in the immediately near future. I think you will agree that I have done my best but it seems to be nugatory in effect and for that I am sorry.

Prompted only by the letters sent by C. R., because at no time, had C.R. ever revealed the full details of his offer, Henry Dyke Dennis wrote to Major Roberts on the 11th March;
I enclose you another letter from Mr. C. R. with regard to the education of the boys which he has offered to take. I really think something should be done one way or the other; either we should write and tell him we don't intend to send any boys, or we should give him the names. You will see from his letter that if he does not hear in the course of a post or two his offer is "off". Personally, I think it is a great pity if they don't take advantage of the education he offers.

Major Roberts wrote to C. R. on the 13th March,(unfortunately this letter is missing from the records) however whatever he wrote, elicited this response from C.R. on 15th March
Gresford Disaster. Education of boys.
Many thanks for your letter of the 13th instant relative to the above, and I am, of course, quite willing to keep the matter open in view of the progress that is being made, and I hope to have the pleasure of hearing more definitely from you in the near future. I wish to help you all I can and as an expert educationist of many years standing hope I may be permitted to do so. All good wishes for what you are doing.

On the 16th March Major Roberts sent a short note to thank C.R. for his " *very patient consideration of their difficulties"*. Not having heard anything more from him for nearly a month, C.R. reiterated on the 12th April " *that he should be glad to know of any developments, to the end in view and to hear when it may be so possible at any rate to interview and examine suitable candidates."* Major Roberts informed him on the 15th

127

April that the Lord Mayor would be attending a meeting in Chester the following day, the Agenda of which contained *"items for the appointment of administrative offices and for the completion of the Trust Deed and Scheme, which were, practically ready for execution, and that the new Secretary would proceed to call meetings of Committees to deal with apprenticeships, education, etc, of dependants of deceased miners... I will take your letter to the meeting and see that the newly appointed Secretary gets into immediate touch with you. You have been very patient indeed."*

The day after this meeting, the 17th April, the new Secretary, E. Williams wrote the following to C.R.

EDUCATION OF BOYS.

Major R.C Roberts, one of the Joint Secretaries of the Fund until yesterday, handed to me your letter dated the 12th inst. immediately was appointed Secretary, and asked me to deal with the same at an early date. I have examined the file and regret to say I am unable to find your original letter containing your offer, therefore I shall be obliged should you kindly let me have a copy of same. Apologising for any inconvenience I may Cause you.

To which, C.R. dashed off two handwritten letters, one to Mr. Williams.

Sir. EDUCATION OF BOYS.

Your letter yesterday. It is much to be regretted that after correspondence having continually passed between myself and the acting Honorary Secretaries since September last, it should now transpire that my original letter and offer was not even kept!! I am away from home and cannot send you an exact copy of the letter in question, but it was to the effect that I should be willing to consider the possibility of being responsible for the cost of education of one or two boys at a Preparatory school of my own in Sussex; subject to my being able to interview them here and their passing satisfactorily tests of mental and physical ability. Do you wish to proceed further with the matter on these lines? It is not a little disheartening to find an offer that I made with the genuine desire to help some of the boys in distress, dealt with so cursorily and very unsatisfactorily. My idea has the support of Mr. H. Dyke Dennis, the Managing Director of the Colliery, and I am informing him of the present unfortunate position. I am nevertheless, still willing to examine such boys here after 7th May, until which date I shall be abroad.

(C.R.also informed Mr. Williams that he had incorrectly spelled his surname!) the other letter was to Henry Dyke Dennis:

Gresford Colliery Disaster. Education of Boys.

You may possibly remember the letters that passed between us on this matter, and the interest I was endeavouring to take. After continual correspondence passing between Major Roberts and myself in communication with it over seven months, I received yesterday a letter from Mr. E. Williams, to whom Major Roberts appeared to have passed the correspondence, to the effect that details of my original offer cannot now be found! What do you think of that as a result of my offer? I have told him nevertheless I am still willing to interview and examine any possible boys, and perhaps you can do something to see that an offer made with the desire to help is not entirely lost.

Henry Dyke Dennis then contacted Mr. Williams enclosing the letter he had received from C.R. on 20th April;

There has been some correspondence between Major R.C. Roberts and a Mr. C. R. with reference to the education of two or three boys (whose fathers were killed in the Disaster) at Mr. R's school. I believe Mr. R. offered to educate the boys for nothing. However, I enclose you a letter I have received from Mr. R, and shall be glad if you will kindly look up the correspondence and reply to him as to whether his offer to educate the boys free will be accepted or not. There has been a lot of correspondence which has been going on for a long time, and Mr. R. is anxious to have the matter settled one way or the other.

Mr. Williams had already written this reply to C.R. on the 20th April:
I am sure that had your kind offer not been based on so genuinely a desire to help those affected through the loss of their fathers in the disaster you would have long since let the matter drop. The Administrative Committee has not yet been completed owing (to)the Denbighshire County Council and the North Wales Coal Owners Association, not having appointed their representatives. I am urging them to do so at an early date, and as soon as the Committee is complete, I shall convene a meeting and deal with your kind offer. May I trouble you to the extent of asking the ages of the boys you wish to be sent to interview. Mr. Williams also informed Henry Dyke Dennis that he was already taking steps to have all the information possible to place before the Committee which he would convene immediately the appointing Authorities had elected their Representatives.

2nd May, C.R. to Mr. E. Williams:
Education of boys. Many thanks for your letter of the 20th ulto, and I would ask your pardon for my seeming discourtesy in not replying earlier,

129

but the delay has been due solely to my temporary absence abroad. I note the position and shall be glad to hear further from you at your kind convenience; and with regard to your last paragraph, I am willing to examine test two types of boys, either those between the ages of say 10 and 12 who might be suitable for schools of a Preparatory type; or those who are already at school but whose education is likely to be affected if they cannot obtain some assistance to that end. I will help all I can.

In reply, on the 3rd May, Mr. E. Williams notified C.R. that
the Administrative Committee would come into force on the 18th May, and that once he had ascertained the necessary information regarding the boys to be educated under the provisions of the Scheme he would, at an early date after, " write you fully and I hope definitely on this matter." C.R. was obliged for the letter and information contained in it and would be interested to hear further from him.

May 20th, Mr. Williams to C.R:
The final meeting of the Original Sub-Committee for the purpose of dealing with matters generally in connection with the dependents of the victims of Gresford Disaster was held on Friday last, when it was reported that the Central Board, London would proceed as soon as possible with a suitable scheme of education for the children of the deceased miners. In view of this, I have obtained the necessary information to enable the Central Board to draft its scheme and find that there are 79 children between the ages of 10 and 15 years. As your kind offer does not come within the provisions of the proposed scheme, I shall be very much obliged should you kindly let me know whether the same includes the whole financial liability or not; if not, to what extent it does. May I ask what the education of the boys you offer to undertake is intended to fit them for in the future, i.e., academic or vocational.

After eight long months of letters being sent back and forth, the last words were had by C.R. One wonders on reading this letter, what had been the point of this lengthy correspondence.
21st May, 1935.

Dear Mr Williams, Education of boys.
I have your letter hereon, which naturally I received with regret, but as you state that my offer does not come within the provisions of the scheme already laid down and determined, is there any use in discussing the matter further? It is not likely that the Committee would consent to diverge from arrangements already agreed.

130

Applications - For a Housekeeper with a view to Marriage.

Of the applications for "a woman to keep house", many came from widowers who were left with young children, "needing a Mother's hand and love," or older widowers with grown up families, other applications were from widows and single women who wanted a companion. One of the earliest letter received, came at the end of November 1934 to the Joint Secretaries from a widower, C.H. of Tunbridge Wells:

Excuse me being so bold in writing to ask you if you have a widow down amongst the victims of the late lamentable disaster, who would like a home and a change up this way. I am a widower having lost my dear Wife last March. I am 64 years old I am in receipt of a Post Office Pension. I am also Relief Attendant at the Corporation Conveniences here receiving £1.4.3 per week (Pay envelope enclosed to verify). I am total abstainer (but not against drink) if anyone likes it. My family are all married and away from home. I have a six roomed house all on my own. I would like to get married again to counteract the loneliness of life.

He gave names and addresses of *"men of standing"* as referees, including a vicar and a Chief Constable, who had known him many years. He was thanked for his letter and told that it would be put before a Committee at their next meeting. The following, neatly written letter dated 17th Oct 1934, was received by the Mayor of Wrexham, also looking for a housekeeper/wife:

Honourable Sir,
Might I ask you if you think you could help me with the following service & at the same time help one of the unfortunate women who have suffered at the recent mine disaster. I might inform you that I am an ex service man age 41, fair, widower, having been unfortunate to lose my wife last March and being left with 8 children one of these the eldest is at service, two smallest are in a home, and three others are expecting to go shortly thus leaving me with 1 boy aged 4 and a half, 1 girl age 13 years. Now the point is this that I want a woman age about 28 to 35 who for the sake of a good home would be willing to keep home for me & look after these two I would prefer a widow if possible and would not object to one child. In fact if she was suitable and was willing I would marry one such person

Another neatly written letter was addressed to Alderman Edward Williams, June 20th 1936 after reading an article concerning *'malicious gossip'* concerning the Gresford Widows.

When perusing the columns of Rednolds this morning, I read with regret the news about the Gresford Widows. It is quite true that one erring person's conduct can be magnified to such an extent, that that thing which we call Human nature, dons a dangerous gossiping cloak, and so persisting does this kind of talk continue, that eventually the cloak is meant to cover All. I can't make myself believe that the vast majority of the Welsh women are less respectful than any others of a different nationality, and it is with this in mind that prompts me to send you this note for this purpose. I am unfortunately a widower, with a family of five, the youngest being 13 years and the oldest 21 years. My own age is 41. I am presently working in the pit, but fortunately I am one of the lucky ones, with a very good income so far as mine wages go. I am Scotch, and take a very keen interest in the big social problems of today, national and international. I am a strict Teetotaller and spend a great deal of my time in studying economics, with an occasional jab at song writing, although I've had no luck in that sphere yet. I have a comfortable home, looked after at the present moment by my daughter who is the oldest, and she is getting married. Wishing not to tread upon your valuable time by writing further details, I just make this request, that you will endeavour to assist me in finding a wife, and being in the position as your in, you will, no doubt be able to classify the respectful and disrespectful Gresford Widows. Needless to say it is one in the first category that I wish. Her age can be from say 33 or so to 40, and I would have no objections if there was one of a family under 14 years. I don't want this to reach the newspapers, and hope that through your secretarial channels you will be able to assist.
P.s. I enclose a photo.

These petitioners and others like them, all received a standard letter from the Secretaries, thanking them for their interest, regardless of their particular request, and assured them it would be put before the appropriate committee at the earliest possible opportunity; but others were informed that *"the matter has been placed before the person in charge of matrimonial affairs, who would communicate with them at a later date."*

Not all the requests for housekeepers were from men, some were from women wanting a housekeeper / companion / nursemaid.

Three days after the disaster a retired lady from Gerrards Cross Buckinghamshire enquired whether there was :.....

"a nice young or middle aged woman, who can cook plainly and is clean and honest, with perhaps one young daughter of about 14".

If so, she could offer them a good home and wages, in return for cooking, housework and help with two young grandsons in the school holidays.

CHAPTER 8
Conclusion

It is possible that we will witness in our lifetime the cessation of all coal-mining and in view of the extremities of the industry we should not regret its end, yet, the experiences and spirit of bravery, loyalty and camaraderie of the men and women who lived and worked in the coalfields of England and Wales will continue to evoke memories and "discussions - about influence, about blame and judgement."

This book I hope illustrates the thinking and the sense of values which maintained not only the mining community of Gresford Colliery but the whole nation in the early 1930's, through its active construction of the past using representative historical documentation (i.e.the letters), not previously used before. It also demonstrates the usefulness of personal testimony to aid the interpretation of documentary evidence and to help confront the absences, not only in the analysis of the material, but also those resulting from unanswered questions, due to what could be seen as the powerful controlling of information.

As each generation of descendants of those miners lost in the Gresford explosion question the why's and wherefore's of what happened in 1934, to understand the relevance of the event, regretfully, there are too few answers. So why bother with this research if that is the case?

I hoped to find some of the missing pieces of the jigsaw that was the mining disaster at Gresford Colliery in 1934.

We do not know for certain what caused the explosion, or how the men died. We know one woman's reaction to the news and the consequences for her and her family from the personal testimony of Blodwen Bryan but we do not have other similar testimonies. What we do have however, are letters which show and tell so much, that have lain 'hidden' in the archives for so many years. The experiences and emotions expressed in the Gresford Letters are the authenticating source of this study.

These letters add to the jigsaw by providing evidence of a response by the nation to a disaster in the 1930's, and show the willingness to help others while suffering themselves. Only by understanding these documents can they be fully appreciated, giving a sense of the life of the period and the particular community of experience. These letters challenge and contradict the 'official' history and enable an 'alternative' version of history to be presented.

If a picture, which is but a mute representation of an object, can give such pleasure, what cannot letters inspire? They have souls, can speak, have in them all that force which expresses the transports of the heart. (Words attributed to Heloise).[66]

The passage of time is the only sense of closure this particular work can have as there are thousands of letters I have not been able to use. Also much more evidence remains untouched in the archives, more pieces to make up the jigsaw of The Mining Disaster at Gresford Colliery in 1934.

Of course there are other perspectives on the Gresford Colliery disaster of 1934. Fact and fiction, local folklore and rumours coalesce to form all sorts of theories about the 'real' cause of the explosion, about the 'exhaustion' of the relief fund and the events and coincidences of that terrible night.
It is difficult without concrete evidence to be sure where reality begins and ends, so I can only hope to that my words and views can add another piece or two to the 'Gresford Jigsaw'.

In the archives there are over ten thousand letters connected to the Gresford Colliey disaster of 1934. I have read them all.

In this work I have tried very hard to show a 'cross-section' of these and to give the reader an idea of the breadth of support (or otherwise) that arrived in Gresford and Wrexham as well as the sheer effort that was required to reply to the letters where necessary, and to administer the money and materials that were donated from all four corners of the world as well as the appeals for help.

Simple space restrictions mean I have been limted in what can be included. In my opinion these last few pages of letters are worthy of being displayed here to 'speak' to you for themselves .... across almost a century of time.

It is my earnest hope that you have enjoyed reading *The Gresford Letters*.

B.Tinson - September 2009

To the committe of the Gresford Disaster
Relief Fund

Dear Sirs

    We the undersigned being the
Survivor's of the great disaster beg to
make an application for a grant from the
above Fund, We recive the sum of £5
Last October, but is was given for us to
get things to replace our cloths which
we had to Leave behind and were given
to understand that our case would
be considered at a later Date, Having
not heard anything we beg to make this
application
Hoping & trusting you will give our case your
earnest consideration & Oblige

        Oblige Yours
      The five Survivors

Mr John El Samuels
3 Quarry Villas
Brynteg
Nr Wrexham

To

Gresford Relief Committee

Sirs

We the Survivors of
the Gresford Disaster do again make an apeal
for a Grant out of the Funds We were promised
that our case would be attended to at a
later date we have apealed twice but we have
heard nothing We are trusting that you will
do your Best for us as we are begining to
think we have been forgoten hoping you will see
us and Oblige yours
The Five Survivors

31/.1./1935

To the Joint Hon. Secretarys, & Committee Gresford
Relief Fund.

Gentlemen,

We the six survivors of the Gresford disaster, do hearby appeal to you for a further grant, as promised some time ago,

We thank you ever so much for what you have done in the past on our behalf, We feel gentlemen having gone through such an ordeal that we require a little more to keep ourselfs fit, in the event of us being offered work either at Gresford or elswere, Having gone through such an ordeal we are still feeling the effects very acutly, And now we understand an attempt is to be made to decend the pit probably work will be resumed in the near future, Therfore gentlemen we want to be ready and more so fit for such a task, Trusting our appeal will not be in vain

We are Gentlemen

John. Edward. Samuals
Albert   Samuals.
Cyril   Chalenal
Thomas.   Fisher
Robert Edw. Andrew.
David   Jones.

You have our. Address's

27th. September, 1934.

Dear Mr. Mayor,

At the meeting of the Hammersmith Metropolitan Borough Council held on Wednesday last, the 26th instant, reference was made to the overwhelming disaster which had recently occurred at the Gresford Colliery, near Wrexham.

The Council had in mind the tragic results of this catastrophe; and I was directed to convey to you, and through you to those concerned, the following resolution:-

"That this Council desires to express its deepest sympathy with the relatives and dependants of those who have lost their lives in the recent terrible colliery disaster near Wrexham."

Believe me, Dear Mr. Mayor,
Yours sincerely,

A Belcham

Mayor.

His Worship the Mayor of Wrexham,
Councillor Herbert Hampson, J.P.,
The Guildhall,
Wrexham, Denbighshire.

NM.

Sept 26th,
Ponion Cottage,
Long Rock Cornwall,

To the Mayor of Wrexham

Dear Sir

I am enclosing a 10/- Postal order
for your fund in aid of the
relatives of the unfortunates in
the terrible disaster, I only wish
that it was much more but
I am only an Old age Pensioner
being 82 years of age and have
put in 60 years work, having first
started work in a Coal mine
before I was 9 years of age

will you please acknowledge
receipt of order and Oblige
yours faithfully

Joan Ap Philo

PO 10/-

19 Iddesleigh Rd.
Queens Park
Bedford.

Oct 9ᵗʰ 1934.

Dear Sir

I am enclosing a P.O.
for 5/- for the relief of the
terrible Colliery disaster we feel
so sorry for the widows and
the children I am 81 years of age.
and went without my dinner
3 days to send this

Yours truly
W. Preston

PO 5/-

Gresford (Wrexham) Colliery Disaster Relief Fund.

Chairman:
COL. ... WILLIAMS WYNN, C.B., T.D., D.S.O.,
Lord Lieutenant of Denbighshire.

Vice-Chairman:
COUNCILLOR H. HAMPSON.

Hon. Treasurer:
SIR H. LL. WATKIN WILLIAMS-WYNN, BART., O.B.

Deputy Hon. Treasurer:
J. W. ROGERS.

Joint Hon. Secretaries:
R. C. ROBERTS.
WILLIAM JONES.

Assistant Hon. Secretaries:
LAWSON TAYLOR.
G. VERNON PRICE.

Imperial Buildings,

Wrexham,

————————— 1935

NAMES AND ADDRESS OF THE ESCAPED MEN.

1. SAMUELS, John Edward.   3 Quarry Villas, Brynteg.

2. SAMUELS, Albert.   11 East Avenue, Rhosddu.

3. CHALLONER, Cyril.   12 Windsor Road, New Broughton.

4. FISHER, Thomas.   71 Trevenna Way, Spring Lodge.

5. ANDREW, Robert Edward.   1 Maes Eithen, Daisy Road, Brynteg

6. JONES, David.   15 Cunliffe Walk, Garden Village.
   (see Allowances paid by post)

142

ALL COMMUNICATIONS TO BE ADDRESSED TO THE COMPANY.

ALL GOODS TO BE CONSIGNED TO GRESFORD COLLIERY SIDINGS, WHEATSHEAF JUNCTION, G.W.R.
ALL OFFERS SUBJECT TO STRIKE CLAUSE AND TO ACCEPTANCE BY RETURN OF POST UNLESS OTHERWISE STATED

The United Westminster & Wrexham Collieries Lim.td

GRESFORD COLLIERY,

Wrexham, 2nd February, 1935.

TELEPHONE Nº 38 GRESFORD.

The Committee,
Gresford Colliery Relief Fund,
County Buildings,
Wrexham.

Dear Sirs,

This is to certify that Gwillym Roberts, 28, Princess

Street, Wrexham, has been in our employ from 1926 up to 1934, when we

very reluctantly had to stop him, owing to having fits, and we considered

it very unsafe for him to be working underground.

Yours faithfully,

W Bonsall

"BRYN ISSA,"
WREXHAM,

.... 5/7/1935.

This is to Certify that G. A. Roberts.

residing at.... 28 Princess Street Wrexham.

is suffering from.... Epileptic attacks ....and is now UNABLE

to follow his occupation.

G K Morgan

....

Skegness Urban District Council.

CLERK,
IVOR M. CULE, (SOLICITOR)
COMMISSIONER FOR OATHS.

ASSISTANT CLERK,
V. H. TIPPET.

TELEPHONE 400-401.

Town Hall,
Skegness, Lincolnshire

31st October, 1934.

The Joint Honorary Secretaries,
    Gresford Colliery Relief Fund,
        County Buildings,
           Wrexham.

Dear Sirs,

<u>Gresford Colliery Relief Fund.</u>

      Your letter of the 29th ultimo has now been considered at the appropriate Committee of my Council, and I am directed to state that they regret that they cannot see their way to take any action in this matter.

Yours faithfully,

Clerk to the Council

P.S. The Council have, however, granted
     a permit for a street collection to
     be made by the Skegness Town Band
     in aid of the Fund.

REPTON RURAL DISTRICT COUNCIL.

ARTHUR E. GILBERT,

CLERK
—

PHONE No. BURTON 3024 (2 LINES).

G/W

Rural District Council Offices,
The Poplars,
Rolleston Road,
Burton-upon-Trent,

23rd October, 1934.

Dear Sirs,

Your letter of the 29th ultimo was considered by my Council at their last Meeting when they directed me to say that as there are already many efforts being made in their District to raise money for the benefit of the Fund they regret they cannot see their way to organise further collections.

Regarding your suggestion that the Council should contribute a donation from their General Rate Fund, the Council feel that as the appeal is meeting with response from the ratepayers generally within the district a contribution from public moneys might prejudice your appeal, and in the circumstances they do not desire to make such a contribution.

The Council desire me to say that they are in deepest sympathy with the dependants in their tragic loss, and that so far as they personally are concerned no effort will be spared to support the cause.

Yours sincerely,

Clerk.

Messrs. R.C.Roberts & Wm.Jones,
Joint Hon. Secretaries,
The Gresford (Wrexham) Colliery Disaster Relief Fund,
County Buildings,
Wrexham.

Civil Service Christmas Toy Appeal.

All Communications to be addressed to
L. J. DE B. REED.

Board of Trade,
S.W.1.

23rd. October, 1934.

Dear Mr. Mayor,

On behalf of my colleagues in His Majesty's Civil
Service, I desire to offer you a supply of toys for the
Children orphaned by the recent sad disaster at the
Gresford Colliery. The number of toys will be about 100
and suitable for children up to about 5 years of age.

I would be much obliged if you would kindly advise me
of the name and address of the person to whom I should
forward the case which may be expected to arrive about
20th - 21st December.

Yours faithfully,

[signature]

The Mayor,
    WREXHAM.

References:

[1] Stuart Hall.1992 maintains is necessary to any cultural study: p. 278 in Gray. 1997.

[2] Miller Jane. Studies in reading Culture.1990

[3] Scott. J. Experience. in Feminists Theorise the Political. Butler. J. & Scott. J. Eds.1992

[4] Kelly I. The North Wales Coalfields A collection of pictures Vol 1. 1990

[5] Jones. J. The Coal Scuttle. 1936. p.21

[6] Gardiner. J. & Wenborn. N. British History. 1995 .p.196.

[7] Lerry. G.G. Collieries of Denbighshire, 1946. p..55.

[8] ibid Lerry

[9] See interview with Ithell Kelly in Ch.5

[10] Ibid Kelly Ch. 5

[11] Ibid Kelly. Ch.5

[12] Williams. C.J. Industry in Clwyd. 1986

[13] Smith. D. Wales between the Wars. Eds. Herbert T and Jones G.E. 1988

[14] Editorial. The Times. 23rd January 1943

[15] Thomas, George. Mr Speaker. The Memoirs of Viscount Tonypandy. 1985. p.24.

[16] Ibid Jones J.

[17] Ibid Kelly I 1990

[18] Ibid Kelly I 1990

[19] Taylor. A.J.P. the Origins of the 2nd World War. 1961. Ch.10

[20] Arnot. R Page. The Miners in Crisis and War. 1961.

[21] 1966, 1967, 1978

[22] Lloyd 1978

[23] Philpott. H R S Daily Herald 24th September 1934

[24] Ibid Kelly ch 5

[25] Ibid Lloyd 1978

[26] Pollard. M. The Hardest Work under Heaven: The Life and death of the British Coalminer. 1984. P.184

[27] Ibid Pollard

[28] Ibid Lloyd 1978

[29] Ibid Pollard 1984 p.166

[30] Ibid Kelly ch 5

[31] Parry Davies. Report Gresford Colliery Explosion 1934. Denbighshire Historical Society Vol.22. 173 p.274

[32] Blodwen: wen Bryan interview Ch 5

[33] Ibid Parry Davies Report

[34] Ibid Kelly ch.5

[35] ibid Kelly ch.5

[36] ibid Kelly ch.5 & Parry Davies Report

[37] ibid Parry Davies

[38] ibid Parry Davies

[39] ibid Kelly ch.5

[40] ibid Kelly ch.5

[41] ibid Kelly

[42] Lloyd

[43] ibid Pollard

[44] ibid Kelly

[45] ibid kelly

[46] ibid Kelly

[47] ibid Lerry G.G.

[48] Gresford Colliery Relief Fund Report 24.9.34 to 31.12.45

[49] Special Correspondent. Daily Dispatch, February 1935.

[50] See ch 5 Interview with Blodwen: wen Bryan

[51] See Gresford Colliery Disaster Relief Fund

[52] Mason Paul. Gresford Colliery Disaster Relief Fund. Chief Archivist's Report. 21986

[53] L.P.Hartley. The Go-Between. 1953. Opening words.

[54] See GCDRF (In Appendices)

[55] Rowbotham, Sheila. Hidden from History : 300 Years of Women's Oppression and the Fight Against It.1973

[56] Geoffrey Barraclough. History in a Changing World,pp.24-5.in Tosh J. The Pursuit of History 1996.

[57] MacMillan, London, 1970

[58] Scott, 1990, p.1

[59] See GCDRF

[60] See ch5 interview with Blodwen: wen Bryan

[61] George Santayana. The Life of Reason, Vol i, ch. 12.

[62] Manchester Guardian 29.9.34.

[63] T.S. Eliot. Four Quartets. Burnt Norton. 1936. Pt.1

[64] Ada Leverson. Tenterhooks. 1912. Ch.7

[65] Empty Cradles. Humphries. M. 1994.

[66] In the foreword by P.D.James. 800 Years of Womens Letters. Olga Kenyon.1992

APPENDICES

List of Appendices

Chronology of the Coal Industry 1912 -1939

1912   First National Coal Strike

1913   Mining disaster at the Universal Colliery, Senghenydd, Mid Glamorgan,killed 439 men and boys on October 14th. This was the worst mining disaster ever to occur in Britain and the latest in a spate of accidents in the Welsh coalfields. Nearly a half of all mining deaths in Britain this year were in Wales. Coal production reached a peak in South Wales with some 56.8 million tons produced by 233,000 miners in 620 pits. In North Wales a further 3.5 million tons were produced at 34 pits by 15.900 miners. Altogether this was some 20 per cent of the British total. This was the year that Barry overtook Cardiff as the world's leading coal exporting port. By now Welsh coal made up one-third of the world's coal exports.

1914-18 The First World War.

1916   South Wales Coalfields taken over by Government.
1919   Royal Commission on Coal Industry recommends nationalisation of industry.
1921   Coal Industry handed back to coal owners, followed by miners defeat in lockout and reduction in wages.
1922   Ending of the post-war boom, beginning of trade slump, unemployment reaches 2 million. Coalition Government of Lloyd George falls.

1925   Britain returns to the Gold Standard, leading to overvaluation of currency and restriction of exports.

1926   GENERAL STRIKE. Crisis in COAL INDUSTRY. Pressure from the National Mineworkers Union for the industry to be nationalised, the mine owners rejected this and demanded longer hours as well as lower wages. With the support of other unions a strike was called which lasted for nine days, when the TUC accepted defeat but the miners continued to strike until November.

1929   Wall Street Crash in U.S. worst time of DEPRESSION.

1931   Labour Government resigns (24 Aug). Replacement National Government removes Britain from Gold Standard (21 Sept) and introduces MEANS TEST, wins General Election (27 Oct).

1933   Unemployment reaches almost 3 million: one in four of working population.

1934   SPECIAL AREAS ACT offers help worth 2 million to most depressed areas.
GRESFORD COLLIERY DISASTER (22 Sept), 266 miners were killed in an explosion.

1935   Continuing unrest in the South Wales coalfield led to one of Britain first 'stay down' strikes at Nine Mile Point Colliery, Cwmfelinfach, Gwent. Some 200 men stayed underground for over two weeks in October.
There were mass demonstrations against the hated MEANS TEST for the payment of poor relief.

1936   Unemployment falls below 2 million for the first time since 1930. JARROW CRUSADE to London to highlight continuing problem of depressed areas.

1939   Outbreak of 2nd World War.1940

Acts of Parliament affecting the Coal Industry

Coal Mines Inspection Act 1850
Passed in the wake of a series of colliery disasters, it provided for the state inspection of the mines on the line already introduced into the textile factories, and imposed minimum standards of lighting and ventilation.

Coal Mines Regulation Act 1860
Prohibited the employment of boys under the age of 12 - or 9-10
if they could produce a certificate of education - and granted the
miners? right to appoint checkweightmen to check the weights of
coal credited to them by colliery officials as a basis for
calculating their piece-work earnings.

Coal Mines Act 1872
Gave protection to checkweightmen, who frequently acted as
Trade Union officials (see Coal Mines regulation Act 1860)
against arbitrary dismissal, though they could still be recruited
only from among the men actually employed in the colliery
concerned. Colliery managers were also required to carry state
certificates of technical competence. Daily safety inspections
were to be carried out, and miners received the statutory right to
appoint (from their own ranks) inspectors who were entitled to
oversee the safety arrangements undertaken by the pit managers.

Coal Mines Regulation Act 1908
Hours of men working underground were regulated to eight hours
- the first time they had been restricted by law.

Coal Mines Minimum Wage Act 1912
Passed in response to the first national coal strike (1912), it
provided for conferences of owners and workers, with
government representatives, to fix the minimum rate of wages in
each district. An aggrieved miner could bring a civil action for
recovery of the minimum wage to which he was entitled.

Coal Mines Act 1930
The working day of the underground miners was limited to seven
and a half hours. It had been reduced to seven in 1920, but
increased to eight again after the failure of the GENERAL
STRIKE in 1926.

THE 1930 COAL MINES ACT

Within a month of the second minority Labour Government coming to
power in 1929 the President of the Board of Trade announced that the
Government intended to take "... powers to compel colliery owners to

conform to the rules of a district organisation, inaugurated with the approval of owners of collieries producing the majority of the output to the district, ... power ... to initiate a scheme in any district which failed to constitute an organisation ... and power to set up a central coordinating authority, if one is not constituted voluntarily.? Notice was thereby served on the coal industry to put its own house in order or else the Government would do so. These measures were incorporated in the COAL MINES ACT 1930.

Although this Act was designed to protect and help those working in the industry its failure lay in its inability to fully grasp the problems it was created to deal with.
Part 1 of the Act dealing with the production, supply and sale of coal, was designed to limit overproduction and price-cutting which kept profits and therefore wages low. A central Council was to periodically assess the Nation's requirements for a given period and then allocate a fixed proportion to each coal producing district. An elected Executive Board would then divide this allocation up between its various collieries. There were penalties to be enforced for exceeding quotas and for the maintenance of minimum prices.

Part 2 allowed for a Commission to be set up ? to further the re-organisation of the coal-mining industry and ... to promote and assist amalgamations where they appear to be in the national interest.? If Owners failed or refused to put forward their own recommendations for re-organisation then the Commission was empowered to do it for them.

Part 3 of the Act decreed that the extension of the miner?s working day by one hour on any day of the year was replaced by an extension of only half an hour. The 8 hour day thus became a 7 and a half hour day, and it was intended that when the 1926 Act expired in 1931 (the working day was increased by one hour to catch up on hours lost through industrial action - General Strike), the maximum should once again become 7, as in 1919.Part 4 of the Act was a relatively unsuccessful attempt to pacify all sides as to who should decide about wages and conditions of work. Whether it should be by the owners or national agreement. Although a compromise was worked out to meet all objections in theory, in practice the Government never tried to enforce it.

PRINCIPAL WELSH COLLIERY DISASTERS FROM ALL CAUSES IN THE YEARS 1913 -1942

Year	Date	Colliery	County	Nature of Disaster	No. Killed
1913	Oct 14	Senghenydd	Mid Glamorgan	Explosion	439
1923	Apr 26	Caldean	Carmarthen	Runaway trams	10
1927	Mar 1	Marine No.1	Monmouth	Explosion	52
1932	Jan 25	Llwynypia No.1	Glamorgan	Explosion	11
1934	Sep 22	Gresford	Denbighshire	Explosion	266
1941	July 10	Rhigos No.4	Glamorgan	Explosion	16

TABLES RELATING TO UNEMPLOYMENT.

Table 1. Percentage rate of unemployment in Great Britain (range each five years) 1900 - 1939

Years	Percentage (annual range)
1900-04	2.5-6.0
1905-09	3.6-7.8
1910-14	2.1-4.7
1915-19	0.4-2.1
1920-24	2.0-14.3
1925-29	9.7-12.5
1930-34	16.0-22.1
1935-39	10.8-15.5

Source: Adapted from A. H. Halsey (ed.), Trends in British Society Since 1900 (London 1972.) 119.

Table 2. Percentage unemployed in the staple trades, 1929 – 1938

Occupational Sector	1929	1932	1936	1938
Coal	18.2	41.2	25.0	22.0
Cotton	14.5	31.1	15.1	27.7
Iron and steel	19.9	48.5	29.5	24.8
Shipbuilding	23..2	59.5	30.6	21.4
Average(all industries)	9.9	22.9	12.5	13.3

Source: J. Stevenson, British Society 1914-45 (Harmondsworth, 1984), 270.

Table 3. Regional variation in unemployment (percentage of insured workers who were unemployed) 1929- 1938

Area	1929	1932	1934	1936	1938
South-east	5.6	14.3	8.7	7.3	7.7
Midlands	9.3	20.1	2.9	9.2	10.0
North-west	13.3	25.8	20.8	13.1	17.7
North-east	13.7	28.5	22.1	16.8	12.9
Scotland	12.7	27.1	23.1	18.7	16.8
Wales	19.3	36.5	32.3	29.4	25.9
Northern Ireland	14.8	27.2	23.4	22.7	24.4
UK (average)	10.4	22.1	16.7	13.2	12.9

Source: G. McCrone, Regional Policy in Britain (London, 1969), 100. The above tables were all taken from: Working-Class Cultures in Britain 1890-1960 Gender, Class and Ethnicity. Bourke,Joanna. 1994. pages 109, 110, 111.

Gresford Colliery Disaster Relief Fund

Correspondence, Donations and Contributions to the Mayor of Wrexham and the Joint Secretaries in aid of the above.

Files 198 to 241 inclusive. Dated September 1934 to February 1935.

Total letters read - approximately 9615

Total money noted as being sent as per the letters read - approximately £235,592

North of England (including a few in Scotland)

Donation

	M	F	Mx	Sch	C	W	Ch
£99,771	947	1658	728	190	595	779	295

South of England (including a few in Devon and Cornwall).

| £56,656 | 711 | 1271 | 639 | 161 | 382 | 641 | 155 |

North Wales

| £17,041 | 198 | 235 | 148 | 46 | 83 | 148 | 149 |

South Wales

| £3,807 | 44 | 71 | 42 | 5 | 59 | 34 | 32 |

Most donations were collected or promised before the closing of funds at the end of November or end of December at the latest. Later donations collected after concerts arrived early in 1935 including £177 from three Councils in South Wales.

Abbreviations

M - Male. (Single signatory).   F - Female. (Single signatory).

Mx - Mixed. including Groups, W I's, Womens Branches of organisations.

Sch - School.   C – Council

W - Works. including Unions and Friendly Societies.
Ch - Church or Chapel.

(following four pages) :
The Gresford Gresford Colliery Disaster Relief Fund Report

THE DISASTER AT THE COLLIERY.

At about 2 a.m. on Saturday, the 24th day of September, 1934, one of the most terrible disasters in the whole history of British Coal Mining occurred at Gresford Colliery, near Wrexham, Denbighshire. At the time there were 428 persons working on the night shift below ground, when in the twinkling of an eye, as a result of a terrible explosion, 266 lost their lives. Some of these men were in the flower of their early manhood; some were mere boys.

At once gallant bands of heroic rescuers volunteered to risk their own lives in a superb effort to save their comrades. It was their task to fight the flames and poisonous gases and they struggled against overwhelming odds to reach those still entombed in other parts of the pit. For 48 hours this work continued without respite, during which time 10 victims had been brought to the surface.

By then, those in charge of rescue operations had reached the definite conclusion that no person in the area affected by the explosion could possibly be alive. This being so and in view of the increasing risk and danger they were reluctantly compelled to order the withdrawal of everyone from the pit. After this had been done the mine was closed down.

The Lord Mayor of London at once left for Gresford to see at first hand the work of rescue and relief.

THE FUND.

The Mayor of Wrexham (Alderman Herbert Hampson) at once opened a Relief Fund which was merged into a more general appeal made by the Lord Lieutenant of Denbighshire (Sir R. W. Williams-Wynn, K.C.B., D.S.O.) This fund including interest reached a total of £275,974 14s. 0d. An official Mansion House Fund was opened by the Acting Lord Mayor of London (Sir Louis Arthur Newton, Bart.) and reached a total of £291,196 11s. 3d.

The first Contributors were His Majesty The King, Her Majesty The Queen and other members of the Royal Family.

4

The two funds included contributions from many local Authorities, the Bank of England, the Joint Stock and private Banks, Insurance Companies, the Stock Exchange, Lloyds and a large number of Companies and business firms. Several Newspapers opened their columns for Contributions to the Funds. The City Livery Companies made generous grants, Churches gave Collections and personal gifts were received in thousands from all over the country. Gifts in kind were also received from New Zealand and English firms. A striking appeal over the B.B.C. was made by Sir Louis Arthur Newton, Bart., (the Acting Lord Mayor of London).

IMMEDIATE RELIEF GIVEN.

A local committee was formed in Wrexham of representatives of Public Authorities, and others under the Chairmanship of the Lord Lieutenant of the County to ensure that immediate relief was afforded to needy dependents. The Clerk of the Peace and the Clerk to the Lieutenancy acted as Honorary Secretaries.

SCHEME OF ADMINISTRATION.

The two Funds having been amalgamated a Trust was declared, a Deed was executed, dated the 30th July, 1935, and the Scheme provided for the widows, children and other dependents of the Victims, or unmarried mothers of children of the victims, and certain employees whose names appear on the books of the Gresford Colliery Company Ltd.

The Fund is administered under the direction of Trustees by a Body of Administrative Trustees (called " the Central Board)" and by a subordinate body (called "the Local Committee ").

5

THE HONORARY ACTUARY'S VALUATION.

The list of dependents having been supplied to the Honorary Actuary, he examined, analysed and tabulated the figures and made recommendations as to grants to sufferers and conditions appertaining to them.

The Honorary Actuary pointed out :—

1. That the principal as well as the revenue of the Fund is to be used to meet the outgoings authorised by the Trust, and the intention is that the whole of the Fund and its income shall be used up during the lifetime of the Beneficiaries, and that they should feel at the same time, that however long they may live and be dependent on the receipt of benefits, those benefits will be fully secured to them.

2. That a number of the Widows were under the age of 30 years, and the operations of the Fund might extend over a period of seventy years or even longer.

3. It might be a permissible course after a period of 50 years (more or less) from the date of the disaster to purchase Annuities for the surviving beneficiaries to provide for them during the remainder of their lives.

GRANTS AND ALLOWANCES.

Made up to the end of 1945.

	£	s.	d.
Dependants Weekly Allowances and Compassionate Grants	183,048	18	4
Medical Fees and Benefits	4,253	5	5
Home-help Grants	515	0	0
Education and Apprenticeship Allowances	5,649	16	2
Old Age Pensioners and Rescue Men	5,835	10	0
Marriage Grants	1,495	0	0
Funeral Grants	1,020	4	0
Mourning	2,693	0	0
Maternity	58	11	0
Grants and Railway Fares to Dependants invited to Holiday Homes	171	10	0
Sundry Unclassified Grants	52	7	7
	£204,793	2	6

6

mourning ... 2,693 0 0
Maternity ... 58 11 0

UNEMPLOYED MINERS.

The Employees of Gresford Colliery who were unemployed consequent upon the disaster were paid weekly allowances, for periods amounting to a total sum of £44,221 19s. 6d. of which £4,025 5s. 0d. was for the purpose of replacing lost tools.

BENEFICIARIES.

Beneficiaries admitted on the Fund are as follows :—

	WIDOWS	CHILDREN	OTHER DEPENDANTS
Total number admitted at commencement of Fund	166	241	209
Total number at end of 1945	93	94	131

In addition to the above there were at the end of 1945, thirty-seven Pensioners receiving Quarterly Allowances.

Cases of special hardship have been, and are being dealt with on compassionate grounds.

PENSIONERS.

130 former employees of Gresford Colliery who attained the age of 65 years and were not re-engaged at the Colliery after the disaster receive a small quarterly allowance but no allowances are paid after 75 years of age.

RE-MARRIAGE OF WIDOWS.

Marriage grants are given and the weekly allowance is continued for six months after re-marriage. If a widow loses her second husband and is in need, she can apply for reinstatement on the Fund, one has been so re-admitted.

MEDICAL SCHEME.

408 widows and children have been provided for under the Fund's Medical Attendance Scheme, which provides for dentures and eyeglasses and treatment by Specialists.

HOME-HELP GRANTS.

13 Beneficiaries who are incapacitated from chronic illnesses receive regular financial assistance towards the cost of home help.

7

the Fund's Medical Attendance Scheme, which provides for

HIGHER EDUCATION.

78 boys and girls have come under the provisions of the Fund's Higher Education Scheme.

Two have reached the University, one of whom has obtained his M.A.

1 (a deaf mute) is receiving suitable pre-vocational training at a Special School.

At the end of 1945 five boys and two girls were receiving higher education.

APPRENTICESHIP.

25 boys have received apprenticeship allowances and 68 boys and girls have received equipment grant.

BOARDED-OUT CHILDREN.

12 orphan boys and girls have been boarded-out with foster parents and 3 by Justices' Orders.

COST OF ADMINISTRATION.

This item has been kept at the minimum having regard to the efficiency required. The annual cost is 7.3 per cent. on the amount of allowances and grants distributed.

IN HIS MAJESTY'S FORCES.

41 boys and girls have joined the Forces, 1 is a Pilot Officer, 1 is a Warrant Officer, 1 is in charge of Army Batteries, 1 in an important position in the R.E. Ordnance Survey Section. Several are N.C.O.'s, and five have made the supreme sacrifice.

CONDUCT.

It is very pleasing to record that when so many young people are brought before the Juvenile Courts, not one instance can be quoted of any of the large number of children connected with the Fund being charged in any shape or form.

8

CONDUCT.

APPRECIATION.

The Central Board through the sympathetic regular contact and guidance of their Visitor are kept in touch with those who are under their care and many grateful letters of thanks have been received from the Beneficiaries.

The Central Board record with deep regret the death of the following Colleagues :—

THE FUTURE.

Beginning with October, 1945, the Central Board has decided, on the recommendation of the Honorary Actuary that the regular beneficiaries of the Fund shall receive a " cost of living " Bonus. There will be a Bonus payment of an extra week's allowance in every month, in addition to which in the month of December 4 extra weeks will be paid, making 5 extra weeks in December. The effect is that in 1946, there will be additional Bonus payments equal to 16 extra weeks of the existing allowances. The intention is that the extra payments should be continued after 1946 if funds permit but this will be a subject for consideration from time to time.

9

be additional Bonus payments equal to 16 extra weeks of the